MW01230911

and

Mrs. C.

To: Priscilla
One of the Best

Why I Am So Proud to Be a Black Man

*The Many Reasons to Uplift and Celebrate
Our Uniqueness in the Universe*

MR. MICHAEL AND MS. C

iUniverse, Inc.
Bloomington

WHY I AM SO PROUD TO BE A BLACK MAN
THE MANY REASONS TO UPLIFT AND CELEBRATE
OUR UNIQUENESS IN THE UNIVERSE

iUniverse books may be ordered through booksellers or by contacting:

iUniverse
1663 Liberty Drive
Bloomington, IN 47403
www.iuniverse.com
1-800-Authors (1-800-288-4677)

ISBN: 978-1-4759-7928-2 (sc)
ISBN: 978-1-4759-7930-5 (hc)
ISBN: 978-1-4759-7929-9 (e)

Library of Congress Control Number: 2013903727

Printed in the United States of America

iUniverse rev. date: 2/27/2013

Table of Contents

Introduction

FIRST LET ME ACKNOWLEDGE that this is *not* a religious text. Now that being said, let's begin.

In the beginning God created (a) man and made him in his image. This man God created was me, a black man. Out of all of the colors in God's world, he created a black man. This man was given dominion over God's world. He was given the knowledge of God's wisdom to name all the animals of this world. By being God's first and only man, he was first in his heart, chosen by God. So my question is how and why have we as God's only chosen people fallen so far away from our standing beside God, who created all that there is in and outside of this world?

Where did we go wrong, trusting man instead of trusting in God? How did we get so lost from our true nature, of being created by God as the first human beings in this world? This man was the first human being to witness his very first sunrise, the first to stand upright and feel the heat of the sun on his face.

He felt the sweat roll down his back as he walked along with God in his garden. He stood in this world in his image, as God had created man. He was the only human known to have walked along with God. As man's new eyes looked over all of God's creations, thoughts from God flooded his soul as to who he was and why he must do God's will.

In the cool of the day, man stood on the ground where his creator walked; he was the shepherd over God's world. He walked amongst the many creatures of God's world and felt the love and peace of God around and through him, tasting for the very first time the life-giving waters of his creations.

He smelled the sweet fragrance of millions of flowers along his path; he knew all of his needs but the most important was feeling the love of God in his soul.

At the end of man's first day, the sun was replaced by the light of the moon and millions of stars. He lay down and a deep sleep fell upon him.

As he slept, God created another human being. From the man's rib he created a woman. His first woman was a black woman. She stood as a beautiful woman, God's gift to the world and man. The man's companion became his soul mate. She was more beautiful than the man could ever have imagined. She reached out her hand to touch his, and at that very moment, the man heard every thought that was in her mind and received the love from her unto his heart. For the first time, he felt his manhood because of the woman. Only God could have created such a miracle.

God's first human creations were given all of his wisdom; there were no boundaries and no fears. This man and woman, God's creations, were unique in ways that no other human could know. This black man was God's very first creation; he was given all his treasures and gifts. God brought forth man, a black man, and from this being, God brought forth a woman, a beautiful black woman.

Man was with God in his spirit when he created the universe and the totality of all things that exist, including heaven and earth. He was here before David. He was here before Moses. He was here before Isaiah. He was here before Israel. He was here before Alexander the Great. He was here before the boy King Tutankhamen, so being the very first black president pales in comparison to being the very first human in the world.

Given all of these truths, how can anyone change God's design or purpose? Who are you to change God's design for his world? Remember, he created this world, not us. These are the facts of our world, not your facts or my facts, only God's. This book is not written as any personal attack on any group or any one person, but these are the facts of our history concerning these truths, not just my opinions.

Many people run and hide from the truths of their acts or those of others. They would rather turn away from the true nature of the facts, cover them up and create lies with a story that comforts them. In other words, they tell lies. Look around you. Look at people today; dog eat dog, cut throat; our politicians, teachers, preachers, doctors, lawyers, parents, best friends, spouses, and this list goes on and on.

The climate of the world today is "I've got mine, the hell with everyone else." Greed is the world's motivating force; you may have encountered a few of these individuals somewhere along the line, maybe even in your own mirror. But when you turn your head away from these wrongful acts or words, you should ask yourself why? We can't even begin to talk about the crushing hatred that our family and friends (and ourselves) carry in their heart and soul, should they have one.

In this book I speak of the inhumane, brutal, horrendous, horrific, criminal acts against a peaceful nation of people who, through force, were brought to this country known as America.

Now I am not saying that all Americans are bad people, for there's bad in every part of this world. Let's just review the facts. Many of you knew of and did nothing about the very evil doings in America. There still exists today an evil hatred in your hearts. This is the America I am writing about. Please don't get the wrong message from my words. Let me be very clear.

There are some black Americans even today from humble beginnings that are filled with this evil and hatred. Let's not forget that it was tribal black people who were capturing their very own people, killing, raping, and selling them over to the slave traders. There's enough blame to go around.

My purpose for this book is to open your eyes and minds and hopefully hearts, by touching souls around the world so people know God's first, primal purpose. Knowing what I know now, I can no longer keep quiet, because every day these words crowd my mind by pressuring my soul.

I must speak these truths and tell these stories of forgotten lives and souls; hopefully, I will be their voice. I just pray to God that I will do the best I can for them. I am the voice for the inhumane crimes that were forced upon them. The same types of things are happening today. I often say I am not trying to change anyone's mind, heart, or opinion.

But we must change. If not, then we as a people will lose all together. From the very beginning, we all came from the same loving God.

Read these pages with an open mind, with the sole purpose of finding your true being, and not as man forced us all to become. Learning these truths will awaken us all so that we will have a clearer vision of ourselves, others, and our planet. If the very first man created by God was a black man and the very first woman was a Black woman, then this would make them the mother and father of mankind. We can make up some other story about our beginnings, but it would be a lie.

My words may hurt, but they are not meant to harm anyone. The truth is always hard to speak, because there have been so many untruths told for so long that the real facts are hard to believe; these secondhand lies are still being bestowed upon the world today.

We as God's chosen people were given as our birthplace the richest land of all, with so many wonderful animals and crystal clear waters. Our homeland has more wealth than the rest of the world combined.

Our homeland is Africa. Even today, after so many others have robbed, stolen, killed, and raped our homeland of her people, Africa's wealth is still untouchable. Behind centuries of atrocities from others (and from some of her own people), she still stands strong. The story I am writing details my people, our people, the people of our beginning. They are just like any other family living upon the land that God created for us all. They started from humble beginnings with grandparents, parents, brothers, and sisters.

They are not any different from any other family in the world. We were in the beginning, just like you, and the only difference was we meant no harm or danger to you. Who can honestly say the same?

PART I. LIFE IN AFRICA

CHAPTER 1

Home

MORNING: AS I RISE from my night sleep while still focusing my eyes, I hear my mother and father's laughter. Then I smell breakfast cooking. As my eyes become clear, I am greeted by my mother's smile. Her smile chases away any nightmares or fears I had during the night. I hear the melody of her voice as she lovingly says good morning and asks how my sleep was. Before I can answer my mother, with perfect timing, my father's voice came thundering over the room; his laughter filled my heart with joy. I feel safe just knowing my parents are here to protect us from any dangers, known and unknown.

After eating breakfast, we have our duties to complete around our village. Everyone does their part and after all is completed the men strike out to hunt for our food. I am too young yet for the hunt. My older brother just turned twelve, and this is his first hunt with our father and the other men in our village. The rest of the younger children work around our village. There are so many other young ones here with me, keeping honor among our homes. We repair what we can while awaiting the safe return of my father, brother, and the other men. We work with our elders by helping them with their animals and learning how to make the clothing for our village. We also learn how to make all of our tools, knives, and cooking pots.

When my father and all the men return from the hunt, I notice a strange look on their faces, but no one speaks of the hunt. After other hunts, the men would tell of their ordeals, yet there was not one whisper about today's adventure. Our father greeted us and cleaned up to prepare for dinner. Our whole village sat down together, giving thanks, and we ate as one. After supper, our elders spoke of our history, the history of our great people. My family was descended from tribal kings and queens. Our father is next to being the king. We learn of our ancestors, who lived, loved, and fought for our future; they lay down their lives for us. They built the homes where we now live.

After the village meeting came to a close, everyone started leaving and going to their homes. As we were leaving, my father was walking ahead of me, my brother, mother, and sister. There was something different about him today. He was holding our mother and sister very close, and when we got home, as always, Father made sure we all were safe and stayed with us. But this night, he had a strange look in his eyes. I had never seen this look from our father before. He kissed all of us good night; he turned to our mother, and then left home.

After my father left, I heard the sound of his footsteps until they reached the distant darkness of the night. I patiently waited for his return, and time seemed to stop. This night was the longest and strangest of my life. We knew that my father was not home with us, and we were as concerned for him as we were about being home alone. He finally returned home, and I felt safe; all was well.

Soon, morning was upon us again, but this particular morning, Father was not here. I wondered whether I had seen our father at home or I had dreamed it.

But before I could ask Mother about Father, she spoke to us; without question, she knew what was on our young minds. In her calming, warm, and soft-spoken voice, she said that Father had work to do and would see us later; we still must do our work around our home, in our garden, and in our village. I then greeted my mother with a morning hug and kiss while holding her close to me. I felt her body tremble with fear, but I knew not to ask about it. She then smiled at me and gave me a morning kiss. Before I could speak to her, my brother and sister were up and the regular sounds of our home were almost back to normal, but for one exception: Father.

After we finished our breakfast, Mother again reminded us of our chores. Yet the strange part of this day was as we went out into our village, we noticed that half of the men were gone. The remaining men were carrying weapons of war. This was a first for all of us.

All of the young boys who normally went on the hunt had stayed in the village. Their job now was to watch over all of the younger children and the elders. We wondered why but dared not question our parents or our elders (this would be looked upon as disrespectful). When our mother and sister headed toward the waterfalls for water, some men had to go along with them as though some harm would come to them.

Usually our village was open, but now it had been enclosed behind a strong wall. Each day fear lived amongst us. We didn't know why there were all of the new changes. Yet without asking, there was a knowledge that danger was coming. It was close and all around us now.

When Father returned with the men from their day of hunting, they carried fewer animals than a regular hunt. Some of the men were very bloody and bruised. Two of the men had to be carried because they were badly hurt, but hurt from what? Never before had our strong men come back like this, with fear on their faces, and only to speak of terror as I have not heard from them before.

When our father arrived home, he stood quietly in the middle of the floor, as though he was reliving the terror that was on his face. Our mother stood along with him. We all stood with them as a family; not one word was spoken. Moments later, Father held all of us, saying how much he loved us and how happy he was to be home again.

Father sat down and Mother started to wash him; as dirt fell away from his body, bruises and cuts appeared all over him. We knew then danger was coming.

Evening finally arrived, and it was time for the village to gather for supper. Everyone was very tense, and all of the men were carrying weapons, which they had never brought to supper before. Now we knew that danger was here all around us. Our father and the elders began to talk about the danger we were now facing. One elder said, "We must tell all about the new dangers which are coming to us. None of our lives will ever be the same. We are facing an enemy all around us as well as our neighboring villages. This enemy kills, robs, rapes, and destroys people's lives. To protect our people, we must be on guard against this new terror."

After the evening meal and our meeting about the dangers, we all headed home. There was still something our father was not telling us. Maybe it was the whole story about his real fears. We reached home, but before I could ask Father about his unspoken fears, Mother spoke to him in her usual loving tone; she asked the same question in a way that he could not refuse her request. He began to tell us about his underlining fears.

Neighboring villagers were not only killing, robbing, and raping, they were also kidnapping people and selling them to slave traders. These kidnapped people were being taken to a new world called the Americas. The fear in my father's voice was still there. I could no longer stay quiet and asked Father what else was troubling him. Because of my fears for his concerns, he answered me. With a troubling tone in his voice, he told us that he had seen one of the slave traders (a foreigner) who were responsible for all of the terror now upon our land. This foreigner was like no other human being Father had ever seen before. He was as white as the clouds in the sky, and his eyes had no life in them.

He was without a soul, but he had one very identifiable trait: as one of the leaders of this pogrom, he held a weapon that looked like a long tree limb; when he pointed it at someone, a very loud noise and flash came from this weapon. Immediately the person it was pointed toward fell dead on the ground with a very big hole in their body.

What kind of weapon could this be? The foreigners were very evil people without human emotions. As I was approaching the age to join the hunt, my father began telling me about the dangers of the hunt, including the other animals that were out hunting for food. We could just as easily become food for them. In other words, they could kill and eat us like we do them. In other words, kill or be killed. Yet now there was a new danger from the foreigners among us. I had to grow up faster than ever and become a man earlier than expected.

I began hunting with father and my brother; we have become prolific hunters as a team. One day on our way home from our daily hunt, we passed a village that had just been raided. Nothing was left standing; no one was left alive. Half of the people were dead or gone, but gone where? We all knew why and how. We were now facing more dangers. We arrived back at our village and were greeted by our people; we were very happy to be safely back home again.

After months with no news of trouble anywhere, we were on our way back from another day's hunt. As we got closer to home, we noticed smoke rising up in the sky from the direction of the village. We dropped our kill from the hunt and ran as fast as our feet could carry us.

As we came closer to our village, we could see smoke and fire rising up. Terror was now in our hearts, and entering what was left of our village brought back the same scene we remembered about all of the other villages we observed after the raiders left. All that was left was death of our loved ones and the destruction of our homes.

We cried out for our loved ones, but there was no sound of any life left. Anger filled our hearts, and my father and the other men gathered together to track down the raiders. Time was against us. We started to follow the trail of these killers. Since the sun was going down, there was not much sunlight left to follow them, but the burning heat in our hearts gave us the strength to go ahead and track them down. Day after day, we trailed after the raiders who had destroyed our homes and kidnapped our people.

One night, after weeks on their trail, we came upon the raiders of our people while they were getting ready for their night's rest. We geared ourselves up in order to attack the raiders, kill them, and take back our people. As night came, time slowed down, and it seemed as if the raiders would never go to sleep.

Just then, five of the raiders, after drinking and drinking, started to rape several of their female captives. Some of the women broke out of their holding straps and started to fight against their captors. While they were fighting for their freedom, our father ran into the camp, yelling at the top of his voice. He put two of the raiders down within seconds. It was so fast that before they could hit the ground, they were certainly dead. We immediately followed behind our king, charging our enemy and fighting until there was not even one of them left alive.

After taking back our people and lining up all of the dead raiders, we noticed one of them was still alive. He was one of the foreigners. This one was very pale; he obviously had no soul. My father and the elders called him a devil. He was the one who had come to our land, bringing death and destruction to our people.

He spoke a very strange language that we could not understand, and we were sure he could not understand us. We all looked at him; we did not know that he was the real reason for the destruction of our people.

Before our father could finish speaking, my brother drew back his spear and gave a mighty thrust, and the head of this devil was off.

Our father then said we would hunt down all of the raiders, the white foreigners, who were making slaves of our people. Our mother and sister were still alive—bruised but alive. Father then took the weapon from the hand of the dead foreigner. This was the weapon that made the loud thundering sound as it killed people.

CHAPTER 2

Cry of a Nation

OUR FATHER BECAME KING of our nation because the raiders had murdered all of the elders. As king, he led the remaining villagers high up into the rugged mountains. Months passed while we were building our new home, which became a fortress from outside dangers. Then came the day when I knew my father had to do what was in his heart and what was in all of our souls. He had to stop the invaders who had brought death and destruction to our nation. Even though we had built a new village far away from all other dangers, it was just a matter of time before our new home would come under attack again. Father also felt that his purpose now was to rid our land of these invaders.

One morning, my father, brother, and a handful of our men said good-bye to their loved ones and left us behind to guard the village. Our king and our men prepared to track and destroy the raiders of our nation because they knew that soon they would come looking for all of us. As our father left, I knew that we would never see him again because of the dangerous journey they were taking.

Days turned into weeks and weeks turned into months. News of our father tracking down the raiders slowly found its way back to us from the people our father and the men rescued from their captors. After being set free by our king and warriors, these people told us stories of how brave and daring they had been in fighting the invaders. We learned about the foreigners from these people who had been saved.

They called themselves Spaniards and Americans. They used other African tribes to capture people and take them as slaves. As more and more new people slowly came into our village, they told us horror stories of people being kidnapped by the invaders.

They said that some people who had been put in shackles by their captors had taken rocks and broke their own hand bones so that they could slip out of their shackles, even cutting off their feet so that they could run away from slavery. They knew that they could die from the large loss of blood. Fathers were killing their whole families rather than letting them face slavery. They fought unto the death against the people who would enslave them. There were many horrible stories that came along with the people who had been saved by our king and men. We called these foreigners devils. The spirits of the people were forlorn until they were saved by our king and his warriors.

YEARS PASS

Eventually, there was less news about our king and his men, and fewer people came into the village after being rescued. The enslavement our people had been going on for many years, but it had never been at this level before. The reason was that more raiders had come to our land, killing, raping, and kidnapping our people and taking them to this new world called the Americas. This new world of people was pushing hard for new slaves to help increase the profits in their new country. They profited from the free labor as well as the sale of slaves.

News now came of war between tribal parties: ethnic cleansing. Roving war parties were killing, raping, and kidnapping people and selling them to the foreign slave traders. There was no peace or rest; it had become very profitable to kidnap and sell other people. Since killing was not profitable, everyone was in danger.

Every day was faced with uncertainties. One day, we went out to hunt for food. We were in the middle of a hunt, but as we began killing our prey, we became the prey. We were surrounded by a very large war party and instantly went into a defense attack mode. We fought for our lives because we had everything to lose. Death was all around us. Men were yelling, blood was everywhere, and the fighting was hard, fast, and long. No matter how many we killed, there were always more of them coming.

The invaders' strength was to overwhelm their enemies with a very large number of warriors. We could no longer fight due to exhaustion.

We tried to save the remaining men so they could live to fight another day, in hopes that we might regain our freedom. We tried to lead these sadistic raiders away from our people.

We became prisoners, and our captors led us away from our home, deep into the unknown, at a very fast pace; there was no rest or stopping. We were not given any food or water; this was to keep us from having any strength so we could not fight back for our freedom. We were taken along an unknown trail into parts of our country we had never seen before. We were far away from our homes and knew that we would never see our family again. We ran all night at a very brisk pace.

Three days had passed, but it seemed as though it was three weeks. As we got closer to the ocean, we could smell the salty water, but there was another scent in the air. When we got closer, the smell became overwhelming. It was the stench of decaying flesh. After arriving, we could hear the cry of a nation. Here there were thousands of families, men, women, young, and old, in shackles, chains, and cages. There were dead bodies all around us. We were now in hell on earth. We were tied down in shackles and given food and water.

Witnessing the rising of the sun on a new day was like the quiet before the storm. The foreigners walked among us, looking us over as if they were shopping for livestock. They began picking out the better specimens from the rest and separating us into groups.

In the middle of this hell-hole, the foreigner kept four large lions in a very large cage. I soon learned why. While we were being fed by our captors, we noticed that the cage had two sections; a set of bars separated the two sides. One of the foreigners pushed a man into one side of the cage. His hands were tied and a hood was over his head. As they locked the cage behind him, they removed the hood from his head and untied his hands.

The look on his face was sheer terror. They removed the middle bars, and just as nature would have it, the lions started to attack this human being. His terrible screams were drowned out by the roaring of the beasts as they tore the man apart in a matter of seconds; eating him alive. The smell of fresh blood filled the air; imagine the horror. The message was very clear. Obey, be very obedient to the slave traders, and give nothing less. Otherwise, then you could suffer the same fate.

We were kept under this horrible fear. We were now facing two devils; one, if we tried to escape and were caught, we would face the lions; two, we were being taken to a foreign land as slaves. We were kept in a series of ocean side cocoons and caves. Ships would appear on the horizon and pull alongside the shore, as other foreigners loaded the lower levels of each ship with as many slaves as it could hold. People were stacked on top of each other, because the slave traders knew half of their precious cargo would die before they reached the Americas.

After two days of loading people, food, and water, the ship would pull away from the loading area. We could feel the movement of the ship on the water. These ships were heading toward the Americas; the trip would take three months.

The living quarters were like packing dead animals on top of each other; it was just too horrible to imagine. Yet people did survive, thank the Lord. People were packed in the belly of these ships and slept on top of each other. The smell was unbearable. People were given rotten food and dirty water. When food supplies ran low, the Americans would chop up the dead slaves and feed them to the live ones down below. The foreigners often raped the females. After they had their way with them, they would throw them overboard into the icy waters. There was a very large group of sharks following these slave ships. They knew they could find plenty of food from these ships; the foreigners would throw dead bodies overboard, and others were fed to the fish just for sport. One could say this was merciful, because they did not have to face the horrors that were awaiting them when they landed in the Americas.

Part II. Movement to America

CHAPTER 3

America

U<small>PON LANDING IN THE</small> foreign land, the precious cargo from the slave ships was unloaded; we were enslaved by our kidnappers. After leaving the ships, we were taken to a very large staging place; many of our people were being held in a very large outdoor camping area. We were cleaned, washed, and fed with all of the food that one could eat. I wondered why we were now given this special care after all the inhumane treatment we received before.

Eventually, we realized that we were being fattened up so that we could be sold for a higher price when the time came. The people that had been here for about two months look healthier and fatter than those of us who just arrived. So after two months of clean water and food, we were just being fattened up for profits. There were thousands of us being sold into slavery as human flesh. After about a month, we heard rumors from some of the people who had been here longer; we were told what to expect and what might happen to us. They always separated families when slaves were being sold. Different people bought slaves for many reasons, even for breeding. You say breeders? Yes, breeders. A breeder would be used to impregnate as many female slaves as possible so that the population would grow for future sales. We were the livestock for the slave owners. Some slaves worked inside the slave owners' houses. Other slaves worked in the fields, toiling from before sunrise to after the sun went down. All the slaves were kept in shacks in a guarded area. This was not the kind of place for any human to live. Some slaves were fed and cleaned, and they were given the trappings of their owners.

After owners cleaned their kill of the day, they would throw away some parts of the animals, such as pig's feet, ears, noses, heads, and guts. The slaves would gather these animal parts up so that they could have food to eat and just survive the day.

In the center of town, the slave traders would sell our people to the highest bidder. Here is where families were separated into other groups; they were never sold together.

Here is where cruelty truly came full circle. Here is where you would never again see your loved ones if they somehow survived the hardship of being captured and taken on the long, agonizing sea trip; families were then sold separately. We were now facing these foreigners in this new land called the Americas. These people were like no other race of people we had ever seen before. This land had thousands of these very pale people with a strange language, hair color, and eyes; they had no souls. Were these real people or had we all died and entered another hell?

All of the people who had been here before us had now been sold; we were next to go on the selling block. By not knowing where we might go next, we were in a true hell. One morning, we were taken out of our cages to be lined up for sale. At that moment, three of our people started fighting for their freedom. All hell broke loose in the town after they escaped. Two of the slave traders were killed by our people fighting for their freedom. We were put back into our cages, and the hunt was on for those who had escaped.

After about two weeks, news came that the runaway slaves had been killed. The Americans brought back the bodies of our people, laid them out in front of us, and then chopped them up into bits and pieces until you could not identify them as human beings. This was another true cruelty of this new world called America. Then the sale of our family began. We were put on a large stage while the buyers stood around us. Slaves were sold to the highest bidder. Our new owner put us in shackles and cages and immediately took us away into the unknown.

My turn then came up. I was put up on this stand where many before me stood, while looking out over the faces of these foreigners, those who would buy my flesh. At that moment, while standing there, this strange feeling engulfed my soul; my mind began to feel the souls of all the people who came before me and had looked out over the faces of these Americans, looking across the wide separation of this land from my homeland.

In my spirit, I could see my home once again. At that very moment, the peace of my father came over me. There was no more fear. The buyers examined each slave before buying them. They would look in their mouths at every tooth, check their tongue and lips, raise their arms, and feel their bones and private parts; they also looked at our feet. Only if we passed their test would they buy the slaves they wanted. We then left with our new owners.

We were loaded in the back of a wagon and tied down like livestock. The ride was rough, hard, and dusty. When we finally reached our new destination, we were covered with so much dust we looked like clay statues. We were led off to our new home. There were slaves here already: house slaves, field slaves, and slaves who cared for other slaves. I was now faced with the decision between running away at the first opportunity that presented itself or staying and living my life out as a slave. Being in a strange country, a new land, not knowing the people or customs, the area, and having no resources or weapons to sustain myself, I decided to stay and wait for the unknown of slavery.

The next morning, our new owner introduced us to the rules of the land: "Obey and you will be fed and kept as a slave. Be disobedient or run away and you will be punished or killed; it's your choice." I was chosen to work in my new master's house. There were two elderly slaves inside, one male and one female. They were in charge of the house slaves and trained them to do their chores. I was now a house Negro, a house slave. My chores were to clean around the house and to serve the master and his family breakfast, lunch, and dinner.

The rest of the new slaves worked in the field, which was a labor of death. The only way you could leave them was by death. They were very hot in the summer and very, very cold during the winter. The shacks that we lived in were just that—shacks; dirt floors, no doors, and barely a roof over our heads. After a long day of working, we tried to make these shacks our new homes. For me, after working in the master's house and looking at the wonderful living conditions that he and his family enjoyed, returning to our shacks let me know that we as slaves were looked upon as less than human. Our sole purpose was to live to serve them at their pleasures up until our deaths.

FIELD NEGRO

Later, I was chosen to work out in the field, picking vegetables and cotton; during the winter months, I cleared the land and built houses. We were given little food and a minimum of clothing. Only half of us had shoes; sometimes, the only way you could get shoes was if someone else died. Our master would decide who would get the shoes.

Working in the field was the hardest type of work, but our people would go to the field in good spirit, with pride and self-respect for their work. Our vegetables were the best you could eat, and the cotton was the cleanest you could buy. But the wear and tear on our bodies brought the ultimate price. We had to use our bare hands and work with bare feet while carrying heavy loads on our backs. Sometimes our mothers, sisters, and wives carried their babies on their backs while working. As soon as our little ones could walk, they worked in the fields. There was no mercy from our daily duties. Year in and year out, all we knew was working for our masters.

Before the rising of the sun, we were working out in the fields, and way after the sun had gone down, we were still working, sometimes well into the darkness. The only way we could have enough food was to take everything the masters threw away. This kept us alive. Sometimes we found dead animals, and they became part of our food too. When our people were too old to work, our master would take them away from the farm and they were never seen again, simply because they needed to eat food and cost the master money. So they had to go, but we wondered where they went. Rumor had it that our masters couldn't sell the older slaves because no one would buy them, and they wouldn't keep them because they were costing them money with no financial return. We found out they were being taken out far away from the farm and killed, and then a big hole was dug and their bodies were dumped into it and covered up.

FEMALE FIELD WORKERS

Women were forced to work beside their men. They had to care for the babies as well as keep working. Our masters cared more about their mules and other animals than they cared for us. Why oh why, what have we done wrong to receive this horrible fate? Our water break meant to keep working until our children brought water out to us; we never stopped moving. We carried large bales of cotton, wheat, and vegetables until darkness. Each night after work, after our meals, the master would come down and take some of our women and rape them over and over; there was nothing we could do to help them or keep them from this evil fate. We would be killed by the white men who called themselves our masters. Sometimes our young children were raped by these same white men, never to be seen again. This life was a living death, but what choices did we have? We were kidnapped people taken to the other side of the world, with no chance of returning back to our home. We must call this place home. This was a monstrous place of hopelessness, a living death.

Why our children? What could our masters want with our children? When our babies finally came back to us, they were never the same; their buttocks were bloody and painful; our children told us these devils had raped them, which caused us more pain in our souls. After hearing of these acts, our people decided to fight back against this terrible crime upon our children and our women. We must kill these monsters or die trying. We had a plan to kill our masters, but when the time came to act the next day, we were put into shackles and carried down to the river and pushed into the cold waters until we were almost dead. The master found out about our plans from one of our people, who turned us in. After a long while, the master pulled our men from the waters and told us that if we even spoke of any harm to any white person, we would be killed and they would replace us as if we never lived before or even existed.

To All Decent People

What would you do if you knew someone was raping your wife, your daughter, your son who is just five years old, or even your newborn? How would you react? Could you continue as if all was well? You would probably lose your mind, but then we all know what you would do to them. Now go back into slavery. What could we do when everyone in your life was owned by your slave masters, and his twelve-year-old son was raping your newborn baby girl, your five-year-old daughter, or even your wife? If you attacked him or even said something, you would be killed. What would you as a decent person do?

By being a slave, the question was already answered: not a damn thing. You may wonder how I know what took place back in slavery times, but you may not care or want to know the truth about America's crimes against God's people. Yet I know you already have all of the right answers, because most of you have the spirit of those people in your family even today; a friend, a mother, father, grandfather, grandmother, or those same people who teach this hatred to others.

History tells us these true stories about the cruelty of slave owners. Black people were held against their will as slaves. Many atrocities were done to them. Let's just think of all the atrocious behavior that was recorded: rape, murder, lynching, and burning. A child's hand was chopped off because he was hungry and ate a piece of carrot from the hot field after working all day. They would work their slaves until their death.

Today, we often hear about someone having sex with a family member or with a child. We all know who we are talking about. Just listen to the news; it's almost always a white male. These are the facts and not my opinions. I could go on and on, but there's no need for me to continue about this subject. Here's my point: Just imagine how bad some of these people are now with laws against these terrible acts. Only in our wildest imagination could we even come close to all of their dark acts against the slaves, when there were no laws, and these same people could rape and murder with a free hand with no one to hold them responsible for their horrible crimes. How long would your decency last before you lost your mind and murdered these people?

CHAPTER 4

Days Turn into Years

YEAR AFTER YEAR PASSES us by. We can now speak our master's language, but we are forbidden from reading, writing, or learning anything other than our work duties. During winter, our master likes to go hunting; killing deer, rabbits, turkeys, and anything that moves in the woods. As the hound dogs run down our master's prey, I run alongside with the hound. On some days, the master has a good kill; on others, not so good. One day, we were in a new hunting ground. The dogs started to run after the rabbits, but they stopped and started to dig in a valley area. As they continued to dig up more of the soil, a strong smell began to fill the air all around me. Just then one of the dogs appeared, with a human hand in his mouth. As he began to chew away at the remaining flesh, I saw to my shock it was from a black person. The rest of the hounds continued to uncover this particular area, as my eyes swelled with fear, shock, and sorrow. There were bodies of many dead slaves; why? How could this be? Who could have done this? These questions clouded my mind, and then all the answers came so clearly and directly to me.

These poor souls had no one to save them. They only had the people who murdered them and cast their bodies in this unmarked grave. I quickly ran to get away from this dark place; I hoped our masters would not catch me here at this burial site, because I would be killed and buried next to the last soul that was already here. After a few moments of terror, the rabbits reappeared and the hounds stopped their digging and started chasing after them; these rabbits may have saved my life by their sacrifice. The master had a good day and killed many rabbits.

While gathering up the kill from the hunt, my soul was still back at the large hidden gravesite of slaves. I must carry their souls with me for the rest of my life. I never forgot that day, because those people were someone's mother, father, sister, brother, baby, or grandparent. But the most sadness for me was that they were human beings in God's eyes and heart.

I never spoke to anyone about this day. The next day everyone kept saying that I was different, not myself. They all asked what happened to me. All I could think to answer was I had a bad headache. I now realized what was waiting for us all: a death and burial in a deep hole. I never again looked at the slave owners or masters as humans; they were subhuman, without souls. I must find freedom at all cost.

At the end of this long day working out in the field, a wagon full of new slaves rolled up. Suddenly, one of the slaves started to fight with the master. As he started running toward the woods, our master aimed and shot this man in the back. But the man did not fall or slow his run. Other masters on horses ran the runaway slave down, and as he lay on the ground under the horses, they stomped him until he was dead. Every bone in his body was broken. It was no longer a noticeable body, just a bloody meat pile. Because of the uprising of slaves against their masters, the slave owners needed help to control them, so they reached out and contacted Willie Lynch, a slave owner from the West Indies.

CHAPTER 5

Willie Lynch: The Making of a Slave

THIS SPEECH IS NOT my own and never could be. To fully express a very important point, the slaves were hated and lived under the most inhumane conditions. This was America from the darkest of darkest of days. The term "lynching" is derived from Lynch's name.

Some of this speech is offensive, but it is necessary for all to know.

This speech was delivered by Willie Lynch on the bank of the James River in the colony of Virginia in 1712. Lynch had been invited to Virginia to masters there his methods of controlling slaves.

GREETINGS

Gentlemen, I greet you here on the bank of the James River in the year of our Lord 1712. First, I shall thank you, the gentleman of the Colony of Virginia, for bringing me here. I am here to help you solve some of your problems with slaves. Your invitation reached me on my modest plantation in the West Indies, where I have experimented with some of the newest and still the oldest methods for control of slaves. Ancient Romans would envy us if my program was implemented. As our boat sailed south on the James River, named for our illustrious king, whose version of the Bible we cherish, I saw enough to know that your problem is not unique. While Rome used cords of wood as crosses for standing human bodies along its highways in great numbers, you are here using the tree and the rope on occasions. I caught the whiff of a dead slave hanging from a tree a couple miles back. You are not only losing valuable stock by hangings, you are having uprisings, slaves are running away, and your crops are sometimes left in the fields too long for maximum profit.

Gentleman, you know what your problems are; I do not need to elaborate. I am not here to enumerate your problems; I am here to introduce you to a method of solving them. In my bag here, I have a foolproof method for controlling your black slaves. I guarantee every one of you that, if installed correctly, it will control your slaves for at least three hundred years. My method is simple. Any member of your family or your overseer can use it. I have outlined a number of differences among the slaves, and I take these differences and make them bigger. I use fear, distrust, and envy for control purposes. These methods have worked on my modest plantation in the West Indies, and it will work throughout the South.

Take this simple little list of differences and think about them. On top of my list is age, but this is only because it starts with an "A." The second is color or shade; then there is intelligence, size, sex, plantation size, status on plantations, attitude of owners, and whether this slave lives in the valley or on a hill, has fine or coarse hair, or is tall or short. Now that you have a list of differences, I should give you an outline of action, but before that, I shall assure you that distrust is stronger than trust and envy stronger than adulation, respect, or admiration. The black slaves, after receiving this indoctrination, shall carry on and will become self-refueling and self-generating for hundreds of years, maybe thousands. Do not forget you must pitch the old black male vs. the young black male, and the young black male against the old black male. You must use the dark-skinned slaves versus the light-skinned slaves, and the light-skinned slaves versus the dark-skinned slaves. You must use the female versus the male and the male versus the female. You must also have your white servants and overseers distrust all blacks. But it is necessary that your slaves trust and depend on us. They must love, respect, and trust only us. Gentleman, these kits are your keys to control. Use them. Have your wives and children use them, never miss an opportunity. If used intensely for one year, the slaves themselves will remain perpetually distrustful. Thank you gentlemen.

LET'S MAKE A SLAVE

It was the interest and business of slaveholders to study human nature, and the slave nature in particular, with a view to practical results. Many of us attained astonishing proficiency in this direction. They had to deal not with earth, wood, and stone, but with men, and by every regard they had for their own safety and prosperity, they needed to know the material on which they were to work. They were conscious of the injustice and wrong they were every hour perpetuating and knew what they themselves would do were they the victims of such wrongs. They were constantly looking for the first signs of the dreaded retribution. They watched, therefore, with skilled and practiced eyes, and learned to read with great accuracy the state of mind and heart of the slave, through his sable face. Unusual sobriety, apparent abstractions, sullenness, and indifference; indeed, any move out of the common was afforded ground for suspicion and inquiry. Frederick Douglass's *Let's Make a Slave* is a study of the scientific process of man breaking and slave making. It describes the rationale and results of the Anglo-Saxon ideas and methods of insuring the master-slave relationship. *Let's Make a Slave; The Origin and Development of a Social Being Called the Negro*. Let us make a slave. What do we need? First of all, we need a black "n-word" man, a pregnant n-word woman, and her baby n-word. Second, we will use the same basic principle that we use in breaking a horse, combined with some more sustaining factors. With horses, we break them from one form of life to another; that is, we reduce them from their natural state in nature. Whereas nature provides them with the natural capacity to take care of their offspring, we break that natural string of independence from them and thereby create a dependency status, so that we may be able to get from them useful production for our business and pleasure.

CARDINAL PRINCIPLES FOR MAKING A NEGRO

Future generations may not understand the principles of breaking both of the beasts together, the n-word and the horse. We understand that short range planning results in periodic economic chaos; to avoid turmoil in the economy, we need long-range, comprehensive planning, articulating both skills and perceptions. We lay down the following principles for long-range economic planning: Horses and n-words are no good to the economy in the wild or natural state. Both must be broken and tied together for orderly production. For an orderly future, special attention must be paid to the female and the youngest offspring. Both must be crossbred to produce a variety of offspring. Both must be taught to respond to a peculiar new language. Psychological and physical instruction of containment must be created for both.

We hold six cardinal principles as self-evident, based upon the following discourse concerning the economics of breaking and tying horses and n-words together, all-inclusive of the six principles laid down. Note: Neither principle alone will suffice for good economics. All principles must be employed for the orderly good of the nation. Accordingly, wild horses and natural n-words are dangerous even if captured, for they will have the tendency to seek their freedom, and in doing so, they might kill you in your sleep. You cannot rest. They sleep while you are awake and are awake while you are asleep. They are dangerous near the family house, and it requires too much labor to watch them away from the house. Above all, you cannot get them to work in this natural state. Hence both the horse and n-word must be broken; that is, breaking them from one form of mental life to another. Keep the body, take the mind. In other words, break the will to resist.

Now, the breaking process is the same for both the horse and the n-word, varying only slightly in degree. But as we said before, there is an art in long-range economic planning. You must keep your eye on the female and the offspring of both the horse and the n-word. A brief discourse in offspring development will shed light on the key to sound economic principles. Pay little attention to the original generation, but concentrate on future generations. Therefore, if you break the female mother, she will break her offspring in its early years of development, and when the offspring is old enough to work, she will deliver it up to you, for her normal female protective tendencies will have been lost in the original breaking process.

For example, take the case of the wild stud horse, a female horse, and an infant horse, and compare the breaking process with two captured n-word males in their natural state, a pregnant n-word woman, and her infant offspring. Take the stud horse and break him for limited containment. Completely break the female horse until she becomes very gentle, where anybody can ride her in her comfort. Breed the mare and the stud until you have the desired offspring. Then you can turn the stud to freedom until you need him again. Train the female horse whereby she will eat out of your hand, as she will in turn train her infant to eat out of your hand also. When it comes to breaking the uncivilized n-word, use the same process, but vary the degree and step up the pressure, so as to achieve a complete reversal of the mind. Take the meanest and the most relentless n-word, strip him of his clothes in front of the remaining male n-words, the female, and the n-word infant, tar and feather him, tie each leg to a different horse faced in opposite directions, set him afire, and beat both horses to pull them apart in front of the remaining n-word. The next step is to take a bullwhip and beat the remaining n-word male to the point of death, in front of the female and the infant. Do not kill him, but put the fear of God in him, for he can be useful for future breeding.

THE BREAKING PROCESS OF THE AFRICAN WOMAN

Take the female and run a series of tests to see if she will submit to your desires willingly. Test her in every way, because she is the most important factor for good economics. If she shows any signs of resistance to submitting completely to your will, do not hesitate to use the bullwhip on her to extract that last bit of b-word out of her. Take care not to kill her, for in doing so, you spoil good economics. When in complete submission, she will train her offspring in their early years to submit to labor when they become of age.

Understanding is the best thing. Therefore, we shall go deeper into the subject matter concerning what we have produced here in this breaking process of the female n-word. We have reversed the relationship and her natural uncivilized state. She would have a strong dependency on the uncivilized n-word male, and she would have a limited protective tendency toward her independent male offspring; she would raise male offspring to be dependent like her. Nature provided for this type of balance. We reversed nature by burning and pulling a civilized n-word apart and bullwhipping the other to the point of death, all in her presence. The ordeal of being left alone, unprotected, with the male image destroyed, caused her to move from her psychological dependent state to a frozen independent state. In this frozen psychological state of independence, she will raise her male and female offspring in reverse roles. For fear of the young male's life, she will psychologically train him to be mentally weak and dependent but physically strong. Because she has become psychologically independent, she will train her female offspring to be psychological independent. What have you got? You have got the n-word woman up front and the n-word man behind and scared. This is a perfect situation of sound sleep and economics.

Before the breaking process, we had to be alert and on guard at all times. Now we can sleep soundly, for out of frozen fear, his woman stands guard for us. He cannot get past her early slave molding process. He is a good tool, now ready to be tied to the horse at a tender age. By the time an n-word boy reaches the age of sixteen, he is soundly broken in and ready for a long life of efficient work and reproducing the labor force. Continually through the breaking of uncivilized savage n-word, by throwing the n-word female savage into a frozen psychological state of independence, by killing of the protective male image, and by creating a submissive, dependent mind of the n-word male slave, we have created an orbiting cycle that turns on its own axis forever, unless a phenomenon occurs and shifts the position of the male and female slaves. We show what we mean by example. Take the case of the two economic slave units and examine them closely.

THE NEGRO MARRIAGE UNIT

We breed two n-word males with two n-word females. Then we take the n-word male away from them and keep them moving and working. Say one n-word female bears an n-word female, and the other bears an n-word male. Both n-word females being life without influence of the n-word male image, frozen with an independent psychology; they will raise their offspring into reverse positions. The one with the female offspring will teach her to be like herself, independent and negotiable (we negotiate with her, through her, by her, negotiates her at will). The one with the n-word male offspring, being frozen in subconscious fear for his life, will raise him to be mentally dependent and weak, but physically strong; in other words, body over mind. Now in a few years, when these two offspring become fertile for early reproduction, we will meet and greet them and continue the cycle. That is good, sound, and long-range comprehensive planning.

Earlier we talked about the noneconomic good of the horse and the n-word in their wild or natural state; we talked about the principle of breaking and tying them together for orderly production. Furthermore, we talked about paying particular attention to the female savage and her offspring for orderly future planning, and then more recently we stated that, by reversing the positions of the male and female savages, we created an orbiting cycle that turns on its own axis forever, unless a phenomenon occurs and shifts positions of the male and female savages. Our experts warned us about the possibility of this phenomenon occurring, for they say that the mind has a strong drive to correct itself over a period of time. They advised us that the best way to deal with the phenomenon is to shave off the brute's mental history and create a multiplicity of phenomena of illusions, so that each illusion will twirl in its own orbit, something similar to floating balls and a vacuum.

Creating a multiplicity of phenomena of illusions entails the principle of crossbreeding the n-word and the horse, as we stated above, the purpose of which is to create a diversified division of labor, thereby creating different levels of labor and different values of illusion at each connecting level of labor. The result is the severance of the points of original beginnings for each illusion. Since we feel that the subject matter may get more complicated as we proceed to lay down our economic plan concerning the purpose, reason, and effect of crossbreeding horses and n-words, we should lay down the following definitions for future generations: orbiting cycle means a thing turning in a given path. Axis means around which a body turns. Phenomenon means something beyond ordinary conception that inspires awe and wonder. Multiplicity means a great number.

Crossbreeding a horse means taking a horse and breeding it with an ass, and you get a dumb backward ass long headed mule that is not productive (or reproductive). Crossbreeding n-words means taking so many drops of good white blood and putting it into as many n-word women as possible, varying the drops by the various tones that you want and then letting them breed with each other until another circle of color appears that you desire. What this means is this: put the n-words and the horse in a breeding pot, mix some assess and some good white blood, and what do you get? You got a multiplicity of colors of ass backward, unusual n-words, running, tied to a backward ass long headed mule.

(The one constant, the other dying, we keep the n-word constant for we may replace the mules for another tool.) Both mule and n-word tied to each other, neither knowing where the other came from and neither productive for itself, nor without each other.

CONTROLLED LANGUAGE

Crossbreeding completed, for further severance from the original beginning, we must completely annihilate the mother tongue of both the new n-word and the new mule and institute a new language that involves their new life's work. Language is a peculiar institution; it leads to the heart of the people. The more a foreigner knows about the language of another country, the more he is able to move through all levels of that society. Therefore, if a foreigner is an enemy of the country, the extent to which he knows the body of the language, the country is vulnerable to attack or invasion by his foreign culture.

For example, if you teach a slave all about your language, he would know all your secrets, and he is then no more a slave, for you cannot fool him any longer, and being a fool is one of the basic ingredients in the maintenance of the slavery system. If you told a slave that he must perform in getting out "our crops," and he knows the language well, he would note that "our crops" does not mean "our crops," and the slavery system would break down, for he will relate on the basis of what "our crops" really meant. You have to be careful in setting up the new language, for the slaves will soon be in your house and talk to you "man-to-man," and that is death to our economic system.

In addition, definitions of terms are only a minute part of the process. Values are created and transported by communication through the body of the language. Society has many interconnected value systems. All the values of the society are bridged by language, which connects them for the orderly working in the society. But for these language bridges, the many value systems would clash sharply and cause internal strife or civil war, the degree of the conflict being determined by the magnitude of the issues. For example, if you put a slave in a hog pen and train him to live there and value it as a way of life, the biggest problem you would have out of him is that he would want you to keep the hog pen clean. If you make a slip and incorporate something into his language whereby he comes to value a house more than he does his hog pen, you've got a problem. He will soon be in your house.

An additional note: Henry Berry, speaking in the Virginia House of Delegates in 1832, described the situation as it existed in many parts of the South at this time: "We have, as far as possible, closed every avenue by which light may enter their [the slaves'] minds. If we could extinguish the capacity to see the light, our work will be complete; they would then be on a level with the beast of the field and we should be safe. I am not certain that we would not do it, if we could find out the process and that on the plea of necessity." (From *Brown America: The Story of a New Race,* by Edwin R. Embree, 1931.)

Let us take these points one by one, because even for white America, these methods not only harm and hold back black people down, they also drag white America down. We are all Americans and joined together by whether our country as a whole becomes the best for us all.

CONTROLLING YOUR BLACK SLAVES

Lynch stated that he had a foolproof method for controlling slaves. I guarantee every one of you that if installed correctly it will control the slaves for at least three hundred years.

Lynch used color for his method, pitting light complexion slaves against dark complexion slaves and having them fight against each other. Even today, this divisiveness is still in effect amongst black people. Here were Lynch's future predictions. We as black people have experienced this method.

I used old against young, young against old. Once again, here is the madness of Lynch's guarantee, keeping black people totally against each other, even between the ages; the young disrespecting their elders and their elders turning their backs against the young.

He used males against females, females against males. When you separate these two units, you have totally destroyed the black family; end of story. Lynch's collateral damage was to a nation.

"Fine hair against coarse hair and course hair against fine hair." To Lynch's credit, he used the vast difference within the black people's gene pool. He was like a mad scientist creating a special formula that turned black slaves into mindless beings; even today this system is still manipulating black people.

"I shall assure you that distrust is stronger than trust and envy stronger than adulation, respect or admiration. The black slaves after receiving this indoctrination shall carry on and will become self-refueling and self-generating for hundreds of years, maybe thousands." Lynch's point is right in front of us all today. Even though he developed his method hundreds of years ago, it is still in full effect today. We as black people continue by our own hands the mind-set of the past; the self-generating mind control actions on ourselves; they are handed down from generation to generation of black people.

He stated you must have your white servants and overseers distrust all blacks. Today, when black people walk into a store, we are followed by the store personnel as if we were criminals. The mistrust toward black people exists even today because Lynch's method also indoctrinated white people with this mindless madness.

"But it is necessary that your slaves trust and depend on us, they must love us, respect and trust only us." This monster is telling all the other monsters to keep blacks down on their hands, keep blacks depending on them; this keeps slaves under us, dependent on whites; wanting black people to respect and trust only whites. They would never give black people respect or trust because they, in their hateful murdering hearts, are better than black people. This is all about control over black people.

"Have your wives and children use them and never miss an opportunity to do so. The slaves themselves will never perpetually trust each other." This was teaching their family to take all and any opportunity to take advantage of blacks and to keep their mistrust ongoing of each other. Lynch told slave owners to keep their feet on their slaves' backs and to take advantage of them at all times. This teaching is still in their mental makeup today; do whatever it takes.

PRINCIPLES FOR LONG-RANGE COMPREHENSIVE ECONOMIC PLANNING

Both horses and n-words are no good to the economy in the wild or in their natural state. Both must be broken and tied together for orderly production.

Black slaves must be broken. In order to break a horse, one must ride on the wild horses' back until it gives in to his master; the horse is converted into a mindless creature. In comparing a slave to a wild horse, the slave must also be broken into a mindless creature, being totally separated from his natural state, under the total control of his master.

If we just open our eyes today, we will observe these methods are still being used; there are black people whose spirits are broken everywhere. This cruel method worked so damn well back in slavery that it's still working today on us all, making some of us remain in a mindless state of existence. Most black people feel that we have arrived. By keeping all blacks in a mindless state, white America creates an economic plan for their benefit.

"For an orderly future, special attention must be paid to the female and the youngest offspring. Both must be taught to respond to a peculiar new language. Psychological and physical instruction of containment must be created for both." This statement from Lynch brings me to anger. So for now I will not give you my answer to this insulting man, but please, from your point of view, let us hear your feelings about this statement regarding our females and our offspring. Now is your time to talk.

BREAKING THE BLACK MAN

"Take the meanest and most restless Negro, strip him of his clothes in front of the remaining male Negroes, the female, and the Negro infant. Tar and feather him, tie each leg to a different horse faced in opposite directions, set him afire, and beat both horses to pull them apart in front of the remaining Negroes. The next step is to take a bullwhip and beat the remaining Negro male to the point of death, in front of the female and the infant. Do not kill him, but put the fear of God in him, for he can be useful for future breeding."

"Breaking the female. If you break the female mother, she will break the offspring in its early years of development. When the offspring is old enough to work, she will deliver it up to you, for her normal female protective tendencies will have been lost in the original breaking process."

"Whereas nature provides them with the natural capacity to take care of the offspring, we break that natural string of independence from them and thereby create a dependency status so that we may be able to get from them useful production for our business and pleasures."

Breaking the black male and the black female along with her offspring is to me the greatest crime against humanity done by this country, along with kidnapping black people and placing them into slavery. These practices are still forced on black people today, just in a more modified upscale model.

FROZEN INDEPENDENT STATE

In this state of independence, she will raise her male and female offspring in reversed roles. For fear of the young male's life, she will psychologically train him to be mentally weak and dependent, but physically strong. Because she has become psychologically independent, she trains her female offspring to be psychologically independent. What have you got? You have the Negro woman out front and the Negro man behind and scared.

CONTROLLED LANGUAGE

We must completely annihilate the mother tongue of the new Negroes. Being a fool is one of the basic ingredients of maintaining the slavery system. For example, if you told a slave that he must perform in getting out our crops, and he knows the language, well he would know that our crops didn't mean our crops, and the slavery system would break down, for he would rotate on the basis of what our crops really meant.

For every black person in America, here is your proof of how we have been under control all these years. This was a perfect form of mind control that started way back in slavery days, and even today, it is still going strong.

Out of fear for her sons and in order to protect them, the female trained them to be mentally weak so that they will never stand up for their women or for themselves to their white slave owners. They would be killed, so the female mother reversed the male roles and trained her daughters to take the lead role. This weakened the men. Today, especially, this is solid proof that the black male is the weakest link in the chain of black people. Out of fear, this frozen independent state has taken away the strength from most black men. So then and now, black women have role reversals without even knowing what was done to them hundreds of years ago. Today we are all fighting a fight against ourselves, which was put in motion a long time ago.

"So you have to be careful in setting up the new language for the slaves who would soon be in your house talking to you as man to man, and that is death to our economic system. For example if you put a slave in a hog pen and train him to live there and incorporate in him to value it as a way of life completely, the biggest problem you would have out of him is that he would want you to keep the hog pen clean. If you make a slip and incorporates something in his language whereby he comes to value a home more that he does his hog pen, and then you've got a problem. He will soon be in your house. We have as far as possible closed every avenue by which light may enter their [the slaves'] minds. If we could extinguish the capacity to see the light, our work would be complete. They would then be on a level with the beast of the field and we should be safe."

Once again, here is the manipulation of our minds. He will never hold a black man as his equal. We were not allowed to talk to the white slave owners, man-to-man, then or even today. We are not respected as men, and they use their vicious controlling language; in other words, lie, lie, lie, trusting the truth; changing all the rules; whatever it takes to keep us in our places; giving us no more to live in than a hog pen and expecting us to be happy, thinking we have everything we need.

They want us to believe they will take care of our every need; so then we will still be like a beast in the field, no more. Systematically they continue to control us even today. We must retrain our minds and stand up for our people. Growing up, I remember seeing a picture of white Jesus in almost every black family's house. Every church had this picture of a white Jesus. We all prayed, looked up to, and worshiped this doctrine. All of our hopes and dreams were praying and looking up to this white Jesus. But here is a question for you: When Jesus was on this earth, there were no cameras to take a picture of him; how did this picture of Jesus come to be in every church and almost every black family's house?

Now let us look closely at this form of mind control by having a picture of a white Jesus. Subconsciously we will worship all white men without questioning their control over us. We are being controlled by this picture of white Jesus in our homes and in our churches. This is a perfect storm of mind control that was started way back by Willie Lynch. It has been upgraded for today's times. We must understand we are constantly under attack. Please understand these points.

There are different groups of Negroes:

House Negro
Field Negro
Go tell it on the mountain Negro
New age Negro
I got to get mines Negro
The worst of the worst Negro
The very scary Negro
By any means Negro

We must be aware of our very own people, even your own family members, because some of them are (and always will be) under the influence of our enemy as informants. This is just the way some of our people are.

CHAPTER 6

Which Presidents Owned Slaves

How CAN ANY HUMAN being want to own another human being and hold them in a servitude state of being? And ask yourself how you would feel about anyone owning another human being and having the "free kill" card at any time. How would you feel about someone owning you or your family members? Then remind yourself about these forefathers.

George Washington: Owned more than 200 slaves; some say as high as 350.

Thomas Jefferson: Owned as many as 200 slaves; his wife brought 100 with her dowry.

James Madison: Drafted the Constitution and had over 100 slaves; had to free them in his will.

James Monroe: Owned around 75 slaves.

Andrew Jackson: Owned about 160 slaves.

John Tyler: Owned 70 slaves.

James Polk: Owned 15 to 25 slaves.

Zachary Taylor: Owned up to 150 slaves.

Other presidents through those years—Martin Van Buren, William Henry Harrison, and Ulysses Grant—all also owned slaves. I recommend that you do some homework yourself.

Please, always check the facts yourself.

DECLARATION OF INDEPENDENCE

The Declaration of the Thirteen United States of America

When, in the course of human events, it becomes necessary for one people to dissolve the political bands which have connected them with another, and to assume among the powers of the earth, the separate and equal station to which the laws of nature and nature's God entitle them, a decent respect to the opinions of mankind requires that they should declare the causes which impel them to the separation.

We hold these truths to be self-evident, that all men are created equal, that they are endowed by their Creator with certain unalienable rights that among these are life, liberty and the pursuit of happiness. To secure these rights, governments are instituted among men, deriving their just powers from the consent of the governed. That whenever any form of government becomes destructive to these ends, it is the right of the people to alter or to abolish it, and to institute new government, laying its foundation on such principles and organizing its powers in such form, as to them shall seem most likely to affect their safety and happiness. Prudence, indeed, will dictate that governments long established should not be changed for lightened and transient causes; and accordingly all experience hath shown that mankind are more disposed to suffer, while evils are sufferable, than to right themselves by abolishing the forms to which they are accustomed. But when a long train of abuses and usurpations, pursuing invariably the same object, evinces a design to reduce them under absolute despotism, it is their right, it is their duty, to throw off such government, and to provide new guards for their future security. Such has been the patient sufferance of these colonies; and such is now the necessity which constrains them to alter their former systems of government.

The history of the present King of Great Britain is a history of repeated injuries and usurpations, all having in direct object the establishment of an absolute tyranny over these states. To prove this, let facts be submitted to a candid world.

WHY WE SHOULD STUDY AND KNOW THE CONSTITUTION

The answer is simple enough: because this Constitution is the most important thing in the lives of every person in the United States. Your way of life is built around it; your government is based upon it; and your rights and privileges as a US citizen are protected by it.

To be ignorant of the Constitution is to be ignorant of all the things your country is and of the truths its people have believed to be above all others in the relationships between human beings and government.

Floyd G. Cullop Cotabato, with seventeen years of experience, is a history teacher in junior and high school in Monroe County, Florida and has consistently advocated to his students how critical knowing the laws of the land are to their safety and wellbeing.

These amendments are a must to know.

Amendment 4
The right of the people to be secure in their persons, houses, papers, and effects, against unreasonable searches and seizures, shall not be violated, and no warrants shall be issued, but upon probable cause, supported by oath or affirmation, and particularly describing the place to be searched, and the persons or things to be seized.

Amendment 5
No person shall be held to answer for a capital or other infamous crime, unless on a presentment or indictment of a grand jury, except in cases arising in the land or naval forces, or in the militia, when in actual service, in time of war or public danger; nor shall any person be subject for the same offense to be twice put in jeopardy of life or limb; nor shall be compelled in any criminal case to be a witness against himself, nor be deprived of life, liberty, or property, without just compensation.

Amendment 8
Excessive bail shall not be required, nor excessive fines imposed, nor cruel and unusual punishments inflicted.

Amendment 13
Section (1) neither slavery nor involuntary servitude, except as a punishment for crime whereof the party shall have been duly convicted, shall exist within the United States, or any place subject to their jurisdiction.

Amendment 14
Section (1) All persons born or naturalized in the United States, and subject to the jurisdiction thereof, are citizens of the United States and of the state wherein they reside. No state shall make or enforce any law which shall abridge the privileges or immunities of citizens of the United States; nor shall any state deprive any person of life, liberty, or property without due process of law; nor deny to any person within its jurisdiction the equal protection of the law.

Amendment 15
Section (1) The rights of citizens of the United States to vote shall not be denied or abridged by the United States or by any state, on account of race, color, or previous condition of servitude.

Amendment 26
Section (1) The rights of citizens of the United States, who are eighteen years or older, to vote shall not be denied or a breached by the United States or any state on account of age.

Because of Willie Lynch playing on the minds of black slaves and twisting lies on words, people today are still twisting words around so badly that they are very confused and lost. But if we know our rights and the truth, we can take a strong stand and not accept these lies from unscrupulous people. We have our rights, given to all Americans, by these documents of truth. It is up to us to know these rights. Therefore, I felt compelled to write them down and inform you. Knowledge is power, so please be informed and stay hungry for it.

CHAPTER 7

Turn of the Century: Watch Night

AFTER BEING ENSLAVED FOR hundreds of years, there were many stolen and lost souls. There was a long war fought between the North and South. The North won and the president enacted laws freeing us from ill-gotten gains of slavery.

EMANCIPATION PROCLAMATION

Abraham Lincoln, by his action of setting the slaves free, paid with his life when he was assassinated. These laws were to become active the next day at exactly the stroke of midnight, and every slave watched the clock in anticipation of their new given freedom. This moment in history was called "Watch Night."

The Emancipation Proclamation was an executive order issued by President Lincoln on January 1, 1863, under his war powers. It proclaimed the freedom of 3.1 million of the nation's 4 million slaves and immediately freed 50,000 of them; the rest were freed as Union armies advanced. On September 22, 1862, Lincoln had announced that he would issue a formal emancipation of all slaves in the Confederate States of America.

The Fugitive Slave Law of 1850 required individuals to return runaway slaves to their owners. During the war, union generals such as Benjamin Butler declared that slaves in occupied areas were contraband of war and accordingly refused to return them. This decision was controversial, because it implied recognition of the Confederacy as a separate nation under international law, a notion that Lincoln steadfastly denied. As a result, he did not promote the contraband designation. Some generals also declared the slaves under their jurisdiction to be free and were replaced when they refused to rescind such declarations.

In March of 1862, Lincoln forbade Union Army officers from returning fugitive slaves. The next month, Congress declared that the federal government would compensate slave owners who freed their slaves. Slaves in the District of Columbia were freed on April 16, 1862, and their owners were compensated. In June 1862, Congress prohibited slavery in United States territories, overturning the 1857 Supreme Court opinion in the Dred Scott case.

Now, where do we go from here? After we were granted our freedom, many of us were confused about our lives. Land owners offered to let freed slaves become sharecroppers by living on their land and working in their fields. The land owners said that they would split the profits, but they were lying. Others just stayed with their former owners. Some left their homes, only to face more danger from the hatred that was before them. These former slaves faced murderous hatred in America simply because they were black. Former slave owners displayed their inhumane hatred of blacks after slavery ended; that demonic spirit had been present during slavery. That spirit is alive and working today.

Many freed slaves left their old plantations and were killed along country roads by white Americans. As the years passed, many more lives were stolen. Yet we still made this country our home. Many slaves left the South and moved north, looking for peace.

As freed black people started to make gains in America, the US Congress and many southern states created new laws against us. At every point of progress, there was a new twist on existing laws. Then there came a new virus. This pestilence came in the form of evil white men hiding behind white hoods with white sheets over their bodies; they called themselves the Ku Klux Klan, a.k.a. KKK.

(Research the album cover of Steel Pulse at info@steelpulse.com.)

Throughout America, the KKK terrorized black people with hateful messages and murder; they lynched blacks, and while their bodies hung from the lynching rope, they were set on fire. There were mass killings where some whites brought their whole family out to watch, as if it was a circus. This virus of the KKK and the new Jim Crow laws were the beginning of segregation, which continued to keep black people down and depressed. We were called the n-word, which was designed to devastate and dehumanize us. This institution was another way to keep black people down. The country that kidnapped us, put us in shackles, enslaved us, worked us without pay, and murdered us still had a bitter hatred for us; it continues even now with the new ways of keeping their feet on our backs. We are not allowed to live anywhere we want, to eat at the same restaurants where whites eat, go to the same schools, or toil in the same workplace.

This list goes on and on throughout America. How can any man support his family by living under these horrible conditions? Yet, through all of this hell, we still continue to survive this murdering hatred. As we only lived in where Americans would allow us to live, we endured the terror of the Ku Klux Klan. The KKK would sneak into a black farmer's house at night and pull the family outside, set their home on fire, and then kill all who remained inside. Night after night, home after home, family after family, there was no peace for us, yet we are still here.

There were many times black men were hunted down like wild animals. Americans called this "coon" hunting. Four hundred years of slavery and a hundred years of KKK, along with Jim Crow laws, gave southern states the free "Kill blacks" card. We have no more protection now than we had when we were in slavery. But our people have proven that we are strong and cannot be destroyed by the most horrible inhumanity against any group of people in human history. Americans even called black people "half human" in the US Constitution; it said that black people were only one third of a person, but then the Fourteenth Amendment made us equal.

In 1930, Thomas Shipp and Abram Smith, two young black men who worked in the John Robinson Show Circus, were accused by a teenager of raping his white girlfriend (this accusation was subsequently found to be a lie). A mob of ten thousand whites took sledgehammers to the county jailhouse doors to get these men; although they were lynched, the girl's uncle saved the life of a third by proclaiming the man's innocence. Photos of the lynching were made into postcards to show off civic pride and white supremacy, but the tortured bodies and grotesquely happy crowds ended up angering and revolting as many as they scared.

These are the same people with a rope in one hand and a Bible in their other hand, and they will be the first ones standing in church every Sunday, praying to their God. Do you see some type of hypocrisy in this scenario? Think about it.

This picture is a mirror reflection of America then and now. Just look into the eyes of this angry mob; cold, stagnant looks with smiles on their faces. One match can start a forest fire. One false word from any white person has sent many black men and women to their deaths. Knowing these truths from history and even today, all it takes is a lie from the lips of a white person, and a poor innocent black soul can end in death or imprisonment.

Take Susan Smith, from South Carolina. In 1994, she accused two black men of carjacking her car while her two children were inside. Immediately, the hunt was on for these two black kidnappers. Many innocent black men were picked up, their daily lives interrupted; some were even placed in lineups. Others were taken in and held until Smith finally admitted that she had lied. She had driven to a lakeside ramp, stepped out of her car, and let it roll into the lake while her two children were strapped inside, drowning them. She had lied and falsely accused two imaginary black men of this horrendous act.

(Research the lynching in Marion, Indiana, on August 7, 1930.)

CHAPTER 8

America Labeled Black People Less Educated Than Whites

AMERICAN OFTEN SAYS BLACK people are less educated and not able to learn like whites because of our cranium size. Well, America, explain how these black people succeeded (but wait, I know what their answer will be: There are always exceptions to the rules, so these people must be exceptions). These are just a small group of people from a larger group of black inventors.

Black Inventors and Their Inventions

Invention	Inventor, Year
Air conditioning unit	Frederick M. Jones, 1949
Almanac	Benjamin Banneker, approx. 1791
Auto cut-off switch	Granville T. Woods, 1839
Auto fishing device	G. Cook, 1899
Automatic gear shift	Richard Spikes, 1932
Baby buggy	W. H. Richardson, 1899
Bicycle frame	l. R. Johnson, 1899
Biscuit cutter	A. P. Ashbourne, 1875
Blood plasma bag	Charles Drew, approx. 1945
Cellular phone	Henry T. Sampson, 1971
Chamber commode	T. Elkins, 1897
Clothes dryer	G.T. Sampson, 1862

Curtain rod	S. R. Scratton, 1889
Curtain rod support	William S. Grant, 1896
Door stop	O. Dorsey, 1878
Dust pan	Lawrence P. Ray, 1897
Egg beater	Willie Johnson, 1884
Elevator	Alexander Miles, 1867
Eye protector	P. Johnson, 1880
Fire escape ladder	J. W. Winters, 1878
Folding bed	L. C. Bailey, 1899
Folding chair	Brody & Surgwar, 1889
Fountain pen	W. B. Purvis, 1890
Furniture caster	O. A. Fisher, approx. 1878
Gas mask	Garret Morgan, 1914
Golf tee	T. Grant, 1899
Hair brush	Lydia O. Newman, 1898
Hand stamp	Walter B. Purvis, 1897
Horse shoe	J. Ricks, 1885
Ice cream scooper	A. L. Cralie, 1897
Improved sugar making	Norbet Rillieux, 1846
Insect destroyer gun	A. C. Richard, 1899
Ironing board	Sarah Boone, 1887
Key chain	F. J. Loudin, 1894
Lantern	Michael C. Harvey, 1884
Lawn mower	L. A. Burr, 1889
Lemon squeezer	J. Thomas White, 1893
Lock	W. A. Martin, 1889
Lubricating cup	Elijah McCoy, 1895
Lunch pail	James Robinson, approx. 1887
Mail box	Paul L. Downing, 1891
Mop	Thomas W. Stewart, 1893
Motor	Frederick M. Jones, 1939
Peanut butter	George W. Carver, approx. 1896
Pencil sharpener	J. L. Love, 1897
Record player arm	Joseph H. Dickenson, 1819
Refrigerator	J. Standard, 1891
Riding saddles	W. D. Davis, 1895
Rolling pin	John W. Reed, approx. 1864

Shampoo headrest	C. O. Bailiff, 1898
Spark plug	Edmond Berger, 1839
Stethoscope	Imhotep, Ancient Egypt
Stove	T. A. Carrington, 1876
Straightening comb	Madam C. J. Walker, approx. 1905
Street sweeper	Charles B. Brooks, 1890
Phone transmitter	Granville T. Woods, 1884
Thermostat control	Frederick M. Jones, 1960
Traffic light	Garrett Morgan, 1923
Tricycle	M. A. Cherry, 1886
Typewriter	Burridge Marshman, 1885

Here are some more famous inventors and inventions:

Jan Ernst Matzeliger (1852–1889). Invented a shoemaking machine that increased shoemaking speed by 900 percent. In 1992, the USPS created a postage stamp in honor of Matzeliger.

Lewis Latimer (1848–1928). Invented an important part of the light bulb: the carbon filament. Latimer worked in the laboratories of both Thomas Edison and Alexander Graham Bell.

Blood Banks. The idea of a blood bank was pioneered by Dr. Charles Richard Drew (1904–1950). Dr. Drew was a surgeon who started the idea of a blood bank and a system for the long term preservation of blood plasma (he found that plasma kept longer than whole blood). His idea revolutionized the medical profession and saved many, many lives. Dr. Drew set up a blood plasma bank at Presbyterian Hospital in New York City. His project was the model for the Red Cross's system of blood banks; he became their first director.

George Washington Carver (1865–1943). He was an American scientist, educator, humanitarian, and former slave. Carver developed hundreds of products from peanuts, sweet potatoes, pecans, and soybeans; his discoveries greatly improved the agricultural output and health of southern farmers. Before this, the only main crop in the South was cotton. The products that Carver invented included a rubber substitute, adhesives, foodstuffs, dyes, and pigments.

George Crum. Invented the potato chip in 1853. He was a native American/African American chef at Moon Lake Lodge, a resort in Saratoga Springs, New York. French fries were popular at the restaurant, and one day a diner complained that the fries were too thick. Although Crum made a thinner batch, the customer was still unsatisfied. Crum finally made fries that were too thin to eat with a fork, hoping to annoy the extremely fussy customer. The customer, surprisingly enough, was happy, and potato chips were invented.

Clatonia Joaquin Dorticus. Dorticus was an African American inventor who received many patents. He invented an apparatus for applying dyes to the sides of the soles and heels of shoes; a machine for embossing or contouring photograph paper; a device that helped develop photographs; and a leak stopper for hoses.

Sarah S. Goode. Invented the folding cabinet bed, a space saver that folded up against the wall into a cabinet. When folded up, it could be used as a desk, complete with compartments for stationery and writing supplies. Goode owned a furniture store in Chicago, and invented the bed for people living in small apartments. Goode's patent was the first one obtained by an African American woman inventor.

Benjamin Banneker. He developed the first clock built in the United States; he also helped to create the layout of the buildings, streets, and monuments for Washington DC.

Sarah Boone. Created a device similar to today's ironing board.

Benjamin Bradley. Created a steam engine powerful enough to drive a warship.

Henry Brown. Created a strongbox for people to store important papers at home.

Patricia Bath. A pioneer in the field of ophthalmology, she created a laser that helped perform cataract surgery.

Andrew Beard. Created the "Jenny coupler," which revolutionized the train industry.

Henry Blair. Invented a seed planter and a corn harvester.

Otis Boykin. Invented several small and inexpensive resistors and developed a control unit for the pacemaker.

Charles Brooks. Developed a truck with brushes to clean debris from city streets, the precursor to the modern street sweeper.

George Carruthers. Invented methods of measuring and detecting ultraviolet light and electromagnetic radiation in space.

Matthew Cherry. Created a vehicle that was the precursor to the modern tricycle; also created a special fender for streetcars.

Joseph Dickinson. Developed, improved, and revised reed organs.

Henry Faulkner. Created a ventilated shoe to help to minimize excessive sweating and prevent blisters and sores on people's feet.

Meredith Gourdine. An Olympic silver medalist in the long jump, he created allergen filtration devices to clean the air in houses as well as in the workplace.

Joseph Hawkins. Improved upon the gridiron design to create metal oven racks.

Willis Johnson. Created the egg beater, which revolutionized the world of cooking.

David Crosthuait. Designed heating installations, the most famous of which was Radio City Music Hall.

Mark Dean. Created numerous devices for personal computer architecture and helped revolutionize the computer industry.

Philip Downing. Created a street letter box for postal customers and later patented an electrical switch for railroads.

Thomas Elkins. Created a refrigerated apparatus for keeping perishable foods as well as a chamber commode.

Philip Emeaguali. Created a process for providing massively scalable processing from networked microprocessors and helped to invent Internet applications.

David Fisher. Made the life of furniture makers easier by creating the joiner's clamp and a furniture caster.

George Grant. A Harvard-trained dentist, he invented several items, most famous of which was an improved golf tee.

Lloyd Hall. Revolutionized the world of food preservation and developed numerous processes for eliminating germs and bacteria from foods, utensils, and tools.

Lonnie Johnson. A rocket scientist, he created one of the favorite toys of the 1990s, the Super Soaker.

Marjorie Joyner. Changed the course of hair care history with her permanent waving machine.

Joseph Lee. Created a bread crumbling machine as well as an automatic bread making machine.

Edward Lewis. Created a spring gun, which curtailed trespassing.

Daniel McCree. Created a portable fire escape that attached to wooden windowsills for home use.

Ben Montgomery. Developed a special propeller that allowed steamboats to navigate in shallow water.

John P. Parker. A conductor on the Underground Railroad, he would later patent a screw for a tobacco press.

Andre Roboucas. Invented an immiscible device that could be projected underwater, the precursor to the torpedo.

Valerie Thomas. Developed a device to produce three-dimensional optical illusions and effects.

Ernest Just. Pioneered the fields of marine biology and zoology, researching parthenogenesis.

Lewis Latimer. After beginning his career drafting the patent application for Alexander Graham Bell's telephone, he developed into a profile inventor and rivaled Thomas Edison in the field of electric lighting.

John Love. Created the precursor to the modern pencil sharpener as well as a plasterer's hood.

Elijah McCoy. Created an automatic lubricating cup that provided oil to moving trains; he was held in such high regard that his inventions were called "the real McCoy."

George Murray. Created a cotton chopping device and later served as a United States congressman.

<u>Robert Pelham.</u> Invented a tabulating device and a tallying machine for the United States Census Bureau.

<u>William Purvis.</u> Invented a fountain pen, bag fastener, hand stamp, and electric railway device.

<u>Lloyd Ray.</u> Created the dustpan.

<u>Albert Richardson.</u> Patented a wooden butter churn, a casket-lowering device, and a home fastener.

<u>Richard Spikes.</u> Invented numerous important devices, from automobile directional signals to the automatic gear shift.

<u>Lewis Temple.</u> Created the Temple's iron, an improvement on the harpoon.

<u>George Alcon.</u> A pioneer in the field of semiconductor research and an aerospace innovator.

<u>Mrs. Henrietta Lacks.</u> A HeLa cell is an immortal cell line used in scientific research. It is one of the oldest and most commonly used human cell lines. The line was derived from cervical cancer cells taken from Henrietta Lacks, a patient who eventually died of cancer in 1951. The cell line was found to be remarkably durable and prolific.

<u>George Otto Gey.</u> The cells were propagated by George Otto Gey shortly before Lacks died. This was the first human cell line to prove successful in vitro, which was a scientific achievement with profound future benefit to medical research. Gey freely donated both the cells and the tools and processes his lab developed to any scientists requesting them, simply for the benefit of science. Neither Lacks nor her family gave Gey permission to harvest the cells, but at that time permission was neither required nor customarily sought. The cells were later commercialized, although never patented in their original form.

In the end there was no requirement to inform a patient or

their relatives about such matters because discarded material, or material obtained during surgery, diagnoses, or therapy, was the property of the physician or medical institution.

Granville Woods. Referred to as the "black Thomas Edison," he was a prolific inventor in the areas of the telegraph, railway electrical systems, and railway safety; he successfully sued Edison and was eventually offered a position with Edison's company.

James West. Created the industry-standard affordable electric microphone.

Daniel Hale Williams. Created the method for and accomplished the first successful open-heart surgery.

Shelby Davidson. Created improvements for adding machines as well as an early coin counting prototype.

Thomas Mensak. Revolutionized the production of fiber optic materials.

Dr. Patricia E. Bath. Invented a method of eye surgery that has helped many blind people to see.

My reason for writing about all of these black inventors and their inventions is because America has stated that due to the size of black people's craniums, they are unable to learn and were therefore looked upon as one third of a human being. I beg to differ based on the evidence presented.

We have seen some of the cornerstone inventions from these wonderful and well-educated human beings. These people's ancestors were kidnapped and stolen from their homeland; brought to this country and sold into slavery; could not speak English; did not know anything about this country; yet despite widespread hatred of them, they gave their hearts and souls to this country. Many talented gifts were derived from their hard work and inventions; if you take any of these inventions away from society, how would the world be affected? For instance, just take away Morgan Garrett's invention, the traffic light. How would driving be affected? Daniel Hale Williams inventing the method for heart surgery; what would happen to the many people in need of this surgery? Dr. Patricia E. Bath's method of eye surgery has helped many blind people to see.

Just think of the millions of souls lost due to slavery, and all of the creations or inventions that were lost because of the cruelty forced upon them. For a moment, just think: from out of these countless minds could have been the cure for cancer and many other diseases and medical breakthroughs. Where in the world would we all be? After all of the racist hatemongering, you may be suffering from a deadly medical problem that they could have cured, making this world a better place for us all, but yet your hatred calls you to murder them all. Their possible discoveries and cures died with them.

I am only expressing my opinion regarding this inhumane method of controlling my people. Still today, these methods are being used on black people, just in a more sinister, substratum way.

1. Fort Mose, FL.
Founded in 1738, Fort Mose, located just north of St. Augustine, is the home of the first free black settlement in the United States. In the fight for control of the New World, Great Britain, Spain, and other European nations relied on African slave labor. The king of Spain issued an edict: any male slave from the British colonies who escaped to the Spanish colony of Florida would be set free, as long as he declared his allegiance to Spain and the Catholic Church. The settlement was abandoned when the British took possession of Florida in 1763.

2. Rosewood, FL
Settled in 1870, this was the site of a massacre that will not be forgotten; it could be considered one of the worst racial incidents in US history. By 1915, Rosewood was a small, predominately black town with a population of just slightly more than three hundred. On New Year's Day in 1923, a young white woman claimed that a black man sexually assaulted her; Rosewood was destroyed by a band of white men searching for the alleged suspect. The number of those killed is still unknown.

3. Seneca Village, NY
Located between 82nd and 89th Streets and Seventh and Eighth

Avenues in Manhattan, this was the first community of prominent black property owners. The New York State Census estimated that about 264 residents lived in Seneca Village between 1825 and 1857. The area consisted of three churches, a school, and several cemeteries. All were razed and the history erased with the development of Central Park.

4. Five Points District, NY
High stakes in lower Manhattan. Today we know it as Wall Street, but from the 1830s to the 1860s, this area was the site of Manhattan's first free black settlement. Located on the five-cornered intersection of what was then Anthony, Cross, Orange, and Little Water Streets, it became known as a notorious slum with its dance halls, bars, gambling, and prostitution. Many blacks fled the area to escape the draft riots of 1863.

5. Weekville, NY
This was a refuge for southerners and northerners. What is now Bedford-Stuyvesant in Brooklyn, Weekville was the second largest community for free blacks prior to the Civil War. James Weeks, a freed slave, purchased a significant amount of land from Henry C. Thompson, another freed slave. Weeks sold property to new residents, who eventually named the community after him. It thrived over the years, becoming home to both southern blacks fleeing slavery and northern blacks escaping the racial violence and draft riots in New York and other cities.

6. Greenwood, OK
In the early 1900s, African Americans settled in Oklahoma, seeking employment and other opportunities in the rich oil fields. Greenwood, part of Tulsa, became home to thriving black businesses; a decade later it earned the moniker "Black Wall Street." But in May 1921, Greenwood faced escalating racial unrest after a young white woman accused a black man of rape. The man wasn't charged, but that didn't stop a white mob from burning down Greenwood, the site of the worst race riot in US history.

7. Freedman's Village, VA
In 1863, the federal government built Freedman's Village on the grounds

of Custer and Lee's estates. There were about fifty houses, each of which was divided to accommodate two families. The settlement was home to some notable residents, including Sojourner Truth, who in 1864 worked as a teacher and helped villagers find jobs. The government closed down the village in 1900. It is now the site of the southern end of Arlington National Cemetery, the Pentagon, and the Navy's annex building.

8. Allensworth, CA

In 1908, Lt. Col. Allen Allensworth and four others set up the California Colony and Home Promoting Association, with the mind-set of establishing the state's first all-black township located on the Santa Fe rail line. By 1914, the town housed a black school district, a judicial system, and a hotel. The town struggled to stay afloat in the face of setbacks, from water supply issues to the railroad closing a stop there. The township is now preserved as Colonel Allensworth State Historic Park.

9. Freedmen's Town, TX

At the end of the Civil War, thousands of slaves purchased land and built their homes along the Buffalo Bayou, dubbing it Freedmen's Town. For six decades the town thrived, with churches, schools, stores, theaters, and jazz spots lining the cobblestone roadways. By the 1920s, it was known as Little Harlem, but the Great Depression caused many to lose their homes. Some longtime residents moved to other Houston neighborhoods; others stayed and watched the community deteriorate. In 1964, Freedmen's was designated a historic district.

10. Davis Bend, MS

A progressive slave town, Davis Bend was a former plantation owned by Joseph Davis, who created a more self-governing community among his 350 slaves. Benjamin Montgomery, one of those slaves, served as the overseer after the war. Davis sold the land on which his plantation was situated to Montgomery for $300 in gold. Montgomery maintained the free cooperative community until the 1880s, but the community fell victim to a poor economy and racial hostility. Montgomery's son, Isaiah, established a new town, Mound Bayou, which exists today.

11. Muchakinock, IA

Muchakinock was home to one of the nation's largest coal mining firms, Consolidated Coal Co. In 1880, J. E. Buxton, superintendent at Consolidated, sent officials to recruit black laborers from Virginia and West Virginia. Black families settled in the town, but by 1900 the coal mines were exhausted, and Consolidated started opening up new camps in Buxton, Iowa.

12. Buxton, IA

While it was a multiethnic community, Buxton was considered a "black man's town" because the number of African American families significantly outweighed that of other ethnic groups. As in Muchakinock, blacks held many key roles in town, including justice of the peace and deputy sheriff. With a black population that reached about five thousand, the town was dubbed "a success" by Booker T. Washington. But soon, demand for coal, the town's principal industry, began to lessen. By 1927 Buxton had lost all of its residents.

13. New Philadelphia, IL

Founded in 1836, New Philadelphia was among the first towns registered by an African American prior to the Civil War. Fran McWhorter, a former Kentucky slave, pulled together money from work and his own enterprises to purchase freedom for himself and his family and buy forty-two acres in southwest Illinois. Before the Civil War, his town was a safe haven for the Underground Railroad. But the Hannibal and Naples railroad bypassed the town, and by the late 1880s, residents started leaving. Today, New Philadelphia is an open field. It was named a national landmark in 2009.

14. Pin Oak Colony, IL

Established in 1818, this small township spread across just 480 acres. It was organized under the Northwest Ordinance of 1787, an act that led to western expansion and excluded slavery. After the Civil War, many residents relocated to other towns.

15. Blackdom, NM

Blackdom, established by Frank and Ella Louise Boyer, was the first all-black settlement in New Mexico. The heyday for the town was around 1908, when there were about three hundred residents. They had set up a post office, blacksmith, stores, a hotel, and the Blackdom Baptist Church, which also served as the schoolhouse. In the 1920s, a severe drought led settlers to abandon the town.

The Amistad Verdict
On March 9, 1841, Joseph Cinque and thirty other surviving Africans jailed since 1839 for mutiny on the Cuban schooner *Amistad* were freed when the US Supreme Court ruled they had been illegally enslaved. It was a victory for abolitionists and for John Quincy Adams, who argued that President Van Buren had no right to return them to Cuba. The survivors returned to Africa in 1842.

Black Seminoles
After 1838, more than five hundred black Seminoles walked with the Seminoles thousands of miles to the Indian Territory in present day Oklahoma. Because of harsh conditions, many blacks and other Seminoles died along this trail from Florida to Oklahoma, also known as the Trail of Tears.

PART III. TRANSITIONS

CHAPTER 9

A Hypothetical Family Story

THIS MISSIVE IS WRITTEN as told to me as a young child and I felt the need to share the story so everyone can benefit from it and maybe pass it on.

I am an eighty-eight-year-old white woman. After I read Michael's book, *Mr. Michael Presents the Five "S," Expressions of Love for My Wife and Spiritual Secrets of Life*, I knew that I needed to tell my family story to him in hopes that he would allow me to express my personal experience with you. Reading about his love for his wife and his spiritual wisdom touched my heart, and I could no longer stay silent.

When I was a little girl, every time my brother and I went over to our grandparents' house for a visit, I was filled with sadness and pain, mainly because my grandfather was very racist. He hated black people deep down in his soul. After every meal, he would talk badly about black people. His son (our father) was bred with this hatred, and so were we, from the beginning of our childhood.

They told us that black people were cursed by God; that they were evil; they couldn't be trusted. If you let a black person touch your skin, you would become black and contract a deadly disease, and then you would die. As I became older, my father and his friends would tell horrible jokes about black people. My brother and I were very close when we were younger, but we grew apart because he was indoctrinated into this blinding hatred by the KKK. Sadly, this has separated us.

My feeling is that all people are God's children. As I grew older, most of my friends were aware of this racism, because it was also taught to their family and friends. Sometimes this was all they talked about. There was a code of silence about this hatred toward black people. Whenever my friends and I talked about our family's racism, most of us ended up in tears, because we were not anything like those who were filled with this hate. We were taught that black men would rape us and kill us. We were told that we must stamp this black disease out by destroying all black people. I left for college, and at the first opportunity, I moved away from the deep, deep South by heading north. I am living on my own around so many different people from all around the world. For the first time in my life, I feel free, like a normal human being.

I have made friends with so many black people, and they are no different from my other friends from around the world. I also haven't caught the "black disease" that my family lied about for so many years. I graduated from college and fell in love with the most wonderful man, and he loved me the same way. Two years after college, we married and now have two wonderful children, Mikey and Casey. My family turned their backs on me for leaving home and going to school out of state. After many years, I received a letter from my brother, Bob. He wrote to say that he was dying and wanted me to come and see him before he expired.

Many thoughts and emotions filled my soul, because my husband is black, and this means my children are biracial. I did not want to expose my children to such a hostile climate, and I knew my family might possibly murder me and my family. A couple of days went by, and my loving husband knew something really heavy was on my mind. I could not keep my brother's letter quiet any longer. We stayed up and talked all night until my husband said that I must go see my brother; we all planned to go together because this was a family matter.

The next day we were back in my old hometown, staying at a hotel. I was amazed at how much had changed. At first I went to the hospital by myself to see Bob. When I arrived at his room, it was very dark and there was a strange strong odor in the air. I walked to his bedside and looked down upon his frail body. My eyes filled with sorrow and pain, and I started crying. Before I could stop crying, he reached up and grabbed my hand. In a quiet voice, he called out to me, saying, "Hello Sister, I have long missed you; how are you?"

All I could do was just look at him; no words came out of my mouth; they were stuck in my throat.

After some time passed, I got myself together and we started talking; time just seemed to fly by. I noticed he was getting tired, so I knew he needed to rest. I said I was leaving, and before I could finish, he started to cry, begging me not to go because he felt that he would never see me again. After we talked a little bit longer, Bob fell off to sleep, and I quietly left the hospital. As I was leaving the hospital, I saw my mother in the lobby. Before I could open my mouth, she started crying and I started crying too. All we could do was hold each other.

We just started talking and talking nonstop. My mother asked me where I was staying, but I didn't tell her my own family was here with me. She did not want to let me out of her sight, so she got into the car with me as I was leaving. We drove over to the hotel, and as we entered the lobby and rode the elevator up to my floor, I was so full of emotions about Bob's condition. I opened the door to my room, and Mikey and Casey immediately ran up and greeted me, saying, "Mommy, Mommy, you are back!"

My husband then greeted me, and as I turned and looked back at my mother, she stood in the doorway, silent. Before I could tell my children that this was their grandmother, Casey said she knew this was her "Bell." She said she knew it because she looked just like her. She ran up to my mother and reached up to grab her hand. Mother immediately bent down, grabbed her only granddaughter, and started to cry all over again. All my mother could say was, "You look just like me." Finally we closed the door and my mother met her new grandchildren as well as her new son-in-law.

Time just flew by, and before we knew it, it was the next day. Mother finally revealed to me that she and my father were no longer living together. It was very sad to hear this. She was not sad as she told me this news. I asked what had gone wrong between them. She paused, stared at me, and said that Father and Grandfather had been found guilty of murder and sent to jail. Grandfather died in jail, and my father was serving a long prison term. We went back to the hospital to see Bob, with everyone tagging along. After entering his dark room, we noticed that the smell was back again. As we all stood around his bed, we called out to him; he gradually opened his eyes and smiled at Mother.

She took his hand. He turned to her and asked where his niece and nephew were. Mother and I just looked at each other, wondering how he could know about them, since he had never seen them before. Just then, Mikey and Casey came close to him, and for the very first time he smiled. He sat up in bed, turned and opened up his arms, grabbed them, and would not let them go. As tears flowed down his face, Casey asked him, "Why are you crying, Uncle Bob?" After hearing her say his name for the very first time, we all started to cry, not from sadness, but from joy. How could Casey know his name, and how could my brother know about my children, whom he had never met? Bob also greeted his new brother-in-law, and from that moment in time, we were all family.

My brother seemed as if he was no longer sick, and Mother was very happy. Visiting hours were over and it was getting very late. We said good night, and Bob was smiling because he was so happy. The next day, we headed to the hospital, and as we walked up to Bob's room, we saw that the door was open. We carefully approached the room and noticed it was bright and smelled so clean. When the door completely opened, Bob was not to be found. We all stopped and looked around, thinking that he might be in the restroom, but he was not.

Right then, a nurse came into the room. She explained that Bob had passed away. She said they were so sorry, but then she said that in his last moments, he was so happy, as if he had accepted his fate. As we left the hospital and walked back to our car, Mikey turned and asked, "Why isn't Uncle Bob leaving with us?" Mother turned to him and explained that he had gone to be with God. Mikey said he knew that, because he saw Uncle Bob leaving the hospital, walking with a man who was holding him by the arm. This man was God. We all just smiled; right at that exact moment, the child had eased all of our hearts.

Mother was now all by herself, so we asked her to come and live with us. After taking care of Bob's burial affairs and arriving back home with Mother, we all are family and as one again. A week later, Mother and I began going through his paperwork and saw his diary. We started to read it, but we had to stop due to the content.

It was all about the killing of black people, lynching and burning them as their bodies hung from ropes. They rode through the black neighborhoods, grabbed them off of the streets, and sold them to hospitals or doctors for body parts. They raped the victims as well as turned children over to the men that loved having sex with children. This was the life of my brother, father, grandfather, and their friends.

These horrors went on for years; Bob wrote that even after all of their deaths, these acts would never stop as long as they passed down this evil racism, as long as there were Negroes walking this earth. But at the end of his diary, he had a change of heart and started to turn away from these evil doers. I had to burn the book, hoping that this evil dividing my family would be forever expelled.

Not only did these evil racists cause the deaths of many people, it also turned the racist people into monsters, and this disease was slowly killing them without their knowledge. This virus of hatred also destroyed many families, as it destroyed mine. Speaking from the heart, we all know someone in our family, our friends, or neighbors that carry this hatred; if they don't change their hearts, then you must separate from them, because what happened to my family will happen to yours.

Please, please walk away from this living family hell, because that is all you would end up with. I left and saved myself, my children, and thank God my mother.

CHAPTER 10

Living in the Shadow of Fear

MANY WHITE FAMILIES LIVE under this fear in their own home. This racist hatred is bred into them; it is basic for white men. I know that not all white men are racist. There are many more good ones than bad ones. I will expound on this in another chapter. Let us get back to the point. This hatred inside white America is so destructive that most white females are afraid to take a stand against their loved ones.

They are so afraid of being ostracized by their family, friends, or neighbors, for if they show any favoritism toward any black person, their husband would become hard to live with. Secondly, they as women would be looked upon as "n-word lovers." There is an unspoken code in white America that all whites must stick together against all other races, especially black people. All of your life, white America, you knew that the sky was blue. The Republicans also know the sky is blue, but once President Obama said that the sky is blue, they now say the sky is green.

Most of the racist machine now agrees with the Republicans that the sky is, in fact, green. They have definitely known all their lives that the sky was blue, but most of white America goes along with this hypocritical lie; they must never ever agree with President Obama. They cannot say a black man is right, so they can't agree with him. So if this shoe fits, then this is you. This is what is so wrong with this country. This hatred in America is about hypocrisy; most people are just involved for themselves and their family.

When First Lady Michelle Obama travelled to France, white

America complained that she was spending taxpayers' money on her trip. When President Obama received a brand new bus, the crybabies were at their worst once again, complaining about how much money had been spent on the bus, but wait. President Obama did not spend a penny for this bus; the Secret Service purchased two buses, one for President Obama and one for Mitt Romney, the Republican candidate for president.

Then their biggest cry was "Here's a black man, not the president, but a black man, charging us a million dollars for a bus." Once again the true nature of their racist hatred is very much alive. This hatred is so strong that they will carry it to their graves. When President Obama and the First Family went on a well-earned Christmas vacation, racist white America started whining and telling lies about how much money the president was spending, but when the true story came out, that the president was spending his own money on their vacation, the crybabies crawled back into their holes, anticipating the next moment to come out and complain. When they have anything to blame on the First Family they become as excited as a mad pack of dogs. This is truly sad in this day and age.

These are the same people (white America) who openly state how much they hate President Obama. When questioned about this, they quickly change their tune by saying, "We don't hate him, and we just disagree with his policy." Right. So how many voiced this same sentiment during the rough eight years under President Bush? Everything wrong was okay during the previous administration, with no public backlash, but now it's okay to degrade and insult the president at every turn. I wonder why now.

After President Obama's State of the Union speech to the nation, you guessed it: The racist 50 percent of white America crawled out again with their ugly complaining regarding the president flying around the country on *Air Force One,* whining again about how much money was being used on fuel. But here are the true facts. Every president flew around the country after their speeches. Yet there was never one person crying out against them or the amount of money spent on fuel.

The only obvious difference is skin color. President Obama is black. It is very sad that this racist hatred still is alive and growing today. These people don't see anything wrong with themselves, but the whole world judges us by their statements and acts.

After President Obama finishes his second term and the new president steps in, the nasty, hateful, racist remarks will escalate; they will encourage the new president to burn everything that those black people used and touched, to do a deep cleaning of the White House so that the smell of black would be totally gone. They will say, "Now we have taken our country back. All America is now healed and safe again." Once again, these are the same sad people who stand in church every Sunday, praying to their God, carrying their Bible, and toting a gun at the same time.

When they speak about the "American people," they are only talking about white America. If anyone can prove that I am wrong, please set the record straight. White America knows more about racism than anyone else, because they live with their racist family members, friends, and lovers, 24/7, 365 days a year.

In corporate back rooms or private clubs, the conversation always turns to black jokes, especially when there are no black people around. It is in their nature to turn against those who are different from them. Even if a black person is a friend of a white person, when it is just the two of them the white friend acts as if they are conjoined twins. But the moment the white friend is with other white people, their attitude changes dramatically, simply because if they acknowledge you, their friends would ostracize them and call them "n-word lovers."

I believe most white Americans would be friends with black Americans, but out of fear of retaliation from those of their own race, they resist any involvement.

Fifty percent of white America cannot resist a strong racist hatred of black America and of anyone who is not just like them. Their whole mind-set is to separate themselves from the rest of America. If they could, they would live the good life and keep the rest of us in poverty and servitude, make us clean their houses and wash their asses, because in their minds they are better than us. They must keep control in their hands. Today, I want you to ask this question: What kind of person wants to have slaves? They see no problem in kidnapping them, raping them, and killing them whenever they want. Well, today those acts are illegal. This means that these people were criminals. Yet, they never paid for their crimes, and we as a people turn our heads and hope it just goes away. There will never come a time of peace from these people - Never.

Most white men have two fears:

1. Losing his woman or daughter to a black man (meaning, putting that black snake inside of her).
2. Having a black man who is his equal, is smarter, or has more money than him.

We cannot live today by yesterday's standards, nor can we live tomorrow by today's standards.

What makes one race of mankind carry so much hatred toward their fellow man in their hearts? This hatred is an addiction burning deep down in their souls.

There are many, many hate groups, but there are thousands of other groups within this race that do not express hatred. Can anyone tell me why there is so much hatred in this one race of people? Even though every opportunity is given to them as a privilege, they still carry this hatred. Why? If these people who are harboring so much hatred deep down in their soul stood before God himself, and God gave them the choice to change their hateful hearts in order to enter heaven or continue with their evil hatred and therefore burn in hell, these racist hatemongers would say to God, "We are not going to change, so show us the door to hell." Hell is not hot enough and does not burn long enough. Everyone else is going to need a reservation for their seat in hell, because it will be filled to the brim with these racist hatemongers.

Let me be clear:

Not all of white America is evil, bad, or against black people; there have been thousands upon thousands of white Americans who stood in place for black people and died for us. We obtained our freedom with their help and sacrifice. This other 50 percent are loving human beings with good hearts. In another chapter I will write about some of the kindest people I have ever met. Some of them are white Americans.

CHAPTER 11

Angry Black Women

TODAY, OUR BEAUTIFUL WOMEN are labeled "angry black women." This is a misconception. Let us go back to slavery times. In her eyes, strong-minded men were killed by her white slave masters in order to keep control over the other slaves. In order to save her sons from a horrible death by the hands of their masters, black women protected her man and sons by standing up for them. This role reversal made black men mentally weaker than women, who were stronger in order to save their men from death. For hundreds of years, beautiful black women took upon their shoulders all of the responsibility of being the head of the family. After centuries of this role reversal, our black women are not angry, but they are just tired and worn out for caring for the whole race. How would you feel if you carried this load on your shoulders for hundreds of years? It is time for us as black men to step up and become the head of our people and lead, as it was designed by God in the beginning. We must take a strong stand for us all.

So for those of you who call black women angry, you should trade places with them and walk in their shoes, and let us see what they will call you. Just pay attention to what we see out in the world. How many times have you seen a black woman walking from the grocery store carrying bags of foods, yet she still has her children along with her? The next time you see her, instead of calling her an angry black woman, just look at her face and you will see how tired she really is. Through all of her pain, she continues to go on, no matter her situation; no matter what her condition is, she would never leave her children.

You must now ask this question: Where is the man who fathered her babies? Many of us have heard of black men pumping their chests about how many children they have fathered, but they do not brag about supporting or caring for all of these children. The weakest link in our black family chain is the mentality of the black male. Our strong black women have carried our people to this point; we must help them and become their strength and love them and give them all a long vacation. Just remain our beautiful queens, which they were designed to be in the beginning by God. The black woman is not angry; she is just worn out. Why can't you see this? If only you would stop thinking of your damn selves and give some thoughts about what black women have endured, then your eyes will open to her and to our place in this world. Just open your eyes. Let us go back to work on history. In every religion, the holy books state that God created man first, then he created woman. After these two, there was no mention of God creating any more human beings. Check your history.

This means that the only two people created by God were Adam and Eve, a black man and a black woman. So we must understand the power of a black woman comes from God. Her strength can only be measured by God, because man alone could never measure her ability and mind-set. Man from the beginning until now has overlooked her because of his own insecurity.

BLACK WOMEN ARE THE ESSENCE OF BEAUTY

As the cliché says, variety is the spice of life. Black women come in so many varieties of beautiful shades. When nature turns the temperature dial up just one degree, black women are at your fingertips, from their own complexions, unequalled.

First, you have white chocolate; nature turns the dial up just one degree and there comes light to medium brown chocolate; another turn of the dial and you get medium brown chestnut; turn up another degree and then comes reddish brown chocolate. As the dial goes all the way up to dark chocolate, we are now at the top of the dial. Now we get deep, dark chocolate; the darker the berry, we all know, the sweeter the juice.

There is a natural beauty within their soft touch that is unmatched. You can put ten women in potato sacks; and if just one is a black woman, have them to walk down the street in the dark of night, and I could pick out that one black woman. When a black woman is in a pair of jeans, you know she fills them out naturally. As she walks toward me, a smile starts at one end of my face and goes straight to the other side. As she walks past me, the smell of her perfume dazzles me. Right at that moment, the only two parts of my body that can even move are my heart rate, as it rises, and my eyes, as they follow her while she walks past; this is pure heaven on earth.

Her mellifluous voice touches my soul. Her eyes are the most gorgeous, loving, and sexiest. Imagine my joy that I could actually see my reflection in those eyes. I love her soft satin skin; but the most wondrous part about her is her natural being.

CHAPTER 12

Twenty-Fourth Golden Dynasty/ Ten Thousand More Years

BEFORE EUROPE CAME INTO existence, Egypt had gone through twenty-four dynasties. These were the people who built all the pyramids and the Sphinx. Even today no one can duplicate, build, or even understand how they completed such highly technical structures. With all of the brightest minds today, it is incredible that no one can explain these wonders.

Yes, these black people from the continent of Africa were master builders. These Africans had mapped the stars and could even tell the weight of the earth. One now one must ask where this knowledge came from. First, before we talk about the pyramids or the Sphinx, can you tell us how they moved the large boulders from their starting point to their final resting place?

The closest locations of these boulders were about five hundred miles away. There were no large trucks or trains. Did they use a large crane? No; in Egypt, there were no roads, just desert and sand. So the sand cannot hold the cranes with the weight of these large boulders. So how did they move these large boulders, some that weighed over one hundred tons?

Even today, we do not have machines or roads that can carry these large weights. Let us take a step back before we talk about moving any of these large boulders, some of which are the size of a locomotive engine. How did these master builders cut and shape these stones? Some of today's great minds say they moved these large boulders by shifting the Nile River closer to the boulders. We are told they then floated them down the Nile where they wanted to build the pyramid, but there is this one problem.

How can anyone move a powerful river with the kind of tools they had available? They would have had to first dig a new riverbed over five hundred miles long and then float the boulders down the Nile River. How did they float one-hundred-ton boulders? Did they use boats? There were no boats large enough to float a camel let alone a boulder weighing hundreds of tons. How deep would a river need to be to carry such a weight? And could you stop a one-hundred-ton boulder floating down a river? How could you lift this boulder out of the river?

These questions are difficult to answer; let us move on to the next level: what was used to raise these boulders up? I guess they utilized ropes and camels, right? There are no answers from any of the so-called experts; only these master builders could tell, and they are no longer around to share this information with us.

Now let's observe what is inside the secret tunnels and pathways of these pyramids; no one can explain it. How did they carve out these tunnels and secret chambers with such precision? How could they see within these long chambers or tunnels before electricity was invented? Somehow they were able to get some form of light to see down into the chambers and tunnels. They did not burn torches, because there was no soot on the walls or ceiling.

My belief is that somewhere between the Sphinx and the three pyramids, the secrets of the master builders are buried inside a secret chamber.

This is where we will learn about the minds and skills of these master builders. These black people used the ability that God gave them. From slavery until today, racist white America has labeled black people as having low intelligence. Here the master builders proved their level of intelligence.

With all the black inventors listed above, I have shown that black people have led the advancement of the entire world. Take away any one of them, and this world would be different. Without selfishness, they gave themselves to the world. Yet we are labeled as less than others and compared to the beasts in the field. If black people are less intelligent, then who were these black inventors? Better yet, where did they come from, because they are not like the black people these hateful 50 percent of white America call ignorant?

Afrique became Africa, and the Nile valley started civilization. They set the standard of performance for the world but did not receive credit for it.

Sheik Abidia Adebeys was a scientist, scholar, lecturer, and author who brought forth the contributions of black Egyptians. He used the pigment from the mummies to prove that blacks were in Egypt.

Imhotep was father of medicine in Egypt 1,800 years before the Greeks.

Egypt was tired and old after the twenty-fourth golden dynasty, and in the south the Nubians came along to help Egypt regain her lead. Egypt and the Nubians ruled another ten thousand years in the sun before the rest of the world just started to walk. The world's first two universities, St. Coree (Timbuktu) and Salamence, were started by black people. With all of these gifts to the world, we are still looked upon as beast of the fields and lied about; our history was blocked from the books of man. Yet even today, we get no fairness or respect from our fellow man.

How could you hide the truth, change the truth, bury the truth, but force American beliefs on the rest of the world? Calling themselves honest, just, and fair is common only when it benefits them and only them.

Let me reiterate my meaning. Not all of white America is part of this frenzied group. They are the ones that are in the middle of the road, and thank God for these other 50 percent of white America that stand for justice, fairness, and the goodness of mankind. They are the pure at heart; their acts of fairness give us all hope for a bright future for the entire world. Without them the frenzied groups would destroy this world and themselves because of their narrow-minded hatred against the rest of God's world.

They even hate God along with their own fellow human beings. Their hatred can only be revealed by us as a nation. The true sadness of these matters is that we hear more about the bad news and negativity than we hear about the good, that white America will win out over all of the hatred of the others. Thank God for these wonderful people.

Today greed, special interest groups, hate groups, and their addiction of having it their way means we cannot expect them to change for the betterment of the country; in essence for us all.

From the beginning of this country, a great percentage of white America has been on every front line of our wars, taking part in freedom marches, standing in the line of fire, and even dying for us all. This is why America is a great country. Let's not forget how we all got here. We, the people, must stop allowing others to separate us with their small-minded differences, which can only destroy us all. We, the people, are the people, for the people, one nation under God, in our homeland together.

This information is very important. There's an underlying spirit in America that doesn't want to talk about her shameful past, to erase the facts from history books, keeping us from her true nature, hoping that old saying of "Out of sight, out of mind" will still prevail. If no one talks about slavery, then soon people will forget about it.

Then it would be as if slavery never happened in this country. Once again, here is some very important information about this country during her darkest moments toward blacks.

JIM CROW LAWS

The Harlem Renaissance grew out of the changes that took place in the African American community after the abolition of slavery. These accelerated as a consequence of World War I and the great social and cultural changes in the early twentieth century. Industrialization attracted people from rural areas to cities and gave rise to a new mass culture. There was a great migration of African Americans to northern cities, which concentrated ambitious people in places where they could encourage each other; World War I had created new industrial work opportunities for tens of thousands of people. Factors leading to the decline of this era include the Great Depression.

Until the end of the Civil War, the majority of African Americans were slaves who lived in the South. After emancipation, African Americans began to strive for civic participation, political equality, and economic and cultural self-determination. By the late 1870s, conservative whites managed to regain power in the South. From 1890 to 1908, they proceeded to pass legislation that disenfranchised most

Negroes and many poor whites, trapping them without representation. They established white supremacist regimes of Jim Crow segregation in the South and one-party bloc voting behind southern Democrats. The conservative whites denied African Americans the exercise of civil and political rights. The region's reliance on an agricultural economy continued to limit opportunities for most people. Negroes were exploited as sharecroppers and laborers. As life in the South became increasingly difficult, African Americans began to migrate north in great numbers.

The African American literary movement arose from a generation that had lived through the gains and losses of Reconstruction after the Civil War. Many of their parents or grandparents had been slaves. Their ancestors had sometimes benefited by paternal investment in social capital, including better than average education. Many in the Harlem Renaissance were part of the great migration out of the South into the Negro neighborhoods of the North and Midwest. African Americans sought a better standard of living from the institutionalized racism in the South.

Others were people of African descent from racially stratified communities in the Caribbean, who came to the United States hoping for a better life. Uniting most of them was their convergence in Harlem, New York City.

Despite the increasing popularity of Negro culture, virulent white racism, often by more recent ethnic immigrants, continued to impact African American communities, even in the North. After the end of World War I, many African American soldiers who fought in segregated units like the Harlem Hill Fighters came home to a nation that did not respect their accomplishments. Race riots and other civil uprisings occurred throughout the United States during the Red Summer of 1919, reflecting economic competition over jobs and housing in many cities, as well as tensions over social territories.

CHAPTER 13

Tears of a Nation

When I was thirteen years old, in Atlanta, Georgia, my eighth grade class was playing outside for physical education, as we did every day. We were all called inside before our time was up. When we got inside our classroom, we were told that the president had been shot and killed. Just then, at that very moment, time seemed to stop. We all had to soak in the news that President John F. Kennedy was dead.

Tears started rolling down my face, and my heart became very heavy. All of my muscles locked up, and I could not move. After a moment, the whole class was crying. The teacher turned on the television, and the news was all about the killing of our president; sadness filled the country. We were let out of school early because of this event. When I arrived home, this heavy weight still followed me.

For the first time in my young life, I became aware of the turbulent times in America. I never again looked at America as my country; it was just America. Ever since that day, I have focused all of my attention on world affairs. The tension was very high in America at this time. Lyndon B. Johnson became president, and my people were fighting for civil rights. Jim Crow laws were strong in the South. The Klan had a free hand to roam and kill black people at will, pulling black people from their homes or cars and lynching them, burning their dead bodies while hanging them from the end of their death ropes. Black people could not even enter the front of any business or eat at the same tables as whites did. Black people could only ride public buses in the back, even if there were empty seats at the front.

Mr. Michael and Ms. C

We were not given any respect from most of white America. Many blacks were killed while standing up against the police and Jim Crow laws. I remember public restroom signs separating black people from white people. Our side of the restroom said "Colored only," and the other side said "White only." Water fountains were also marked this way. In those days, there were many strong black leaders who held the black community together with great dignity. In the South, this hatred was at its strongest.

There were many marches in southern cities. One Sunday morning in Alabama, four beautiful black girls were attending church and were killed by a bomb exploded by a white hate group. This is just one out of so many acts that were forced upon black people due to the hatred of America.

These racist people had no fear of our country's own laws. Death and hatred became a part of every black person's psyche. Yet we as a community continued to stand up for everyone's civil rights as human beings and as citizens of America. No matter how many of us were killed, beaten, robbed, or raped, we felt we must keep fighting for justice for all. We were not allowed to attend the same schools as white children; we were not allowed to live in the same neighborhoods. We had no protection from the laws, because white people made the laws. We were still looked upon as subhuman beings without rights.

THE MARCH FROM SELMA TO MONTGOMERY

The death of Jimmie Lee Jackson inspired this monumental march. In 1965, black leaders held a meeting in Zion United Methodist Church in Marion, Alabama; as they sang freedom songs, a league of Alabama State troopers descended upon the church. Jackson and his family ran down to a nearby café for safety, followed by as many as ten troopers. When the troopers started to attack his mother and grandfather, Jackson tried to protect his family. He was shot by James Bonard Fowler and then severely beaten by other state troopers. He was carried to the county hospital where he worked, but the hospital would not treat him, so he was carried to another hospital, Good Samaritan Center; eight days later, Jackson died from his injuries.

Dr. William Dinkins, one of only two black doctors at Good Samaritan, said that Jackson was getting better; he was sitting up and walking around. Someone else said that he was talking too much, and two white doctors said that he needed another operation. Dr. Dinkins argued against this operation, but the white doctors overruled him. During the operation, Jackson died from an overdose of anesthesia.

Saddened by the killing of Jimmie Lee Jackson, black leaders began to plan a march from Selma to Montgomery to petition for a redress of wrongs by the state of Alabama.

There were two attempts to march to Montgomery; the first was known as Bloody Sunday, as a result of the brutal beatings heaped upon marchers by state troopers and others on horseback. On March 21, 1965, protected by federalized National Guard troops, marchers left Selma and arrived in Montgomery four days later, after walking fifty-four miles. Marchers camped out at the City of St. Jude, a Catholic complex that served the black community. On March 24, a tremendously motivating "Stars for Freedom" rally was held on the campus. Singers Harry Belafonte; Sammy Davis Jr.; Peter, Paul, and Mary; and Tony Bennett and Susan Sarandon (18 years old) were all in attendance.

On the following morning, March 25, the marchers completed the last leg of the trek to the state capital. There, Martin Luther King Jr. delivered a powerful speech, "How Long? Not Long." After that march, Mrs. Viola Luzon was giving marchers rides back and forth to their needed locations. As she drove back on a deserted road, the Ku Klux Klan drove alongside her and shot her in her head twice; she died along the side of the road in her car all alone.

The Selma to Montgomery march effected great change in Alabama and the nation. On August 6, President Lyndon B. Johnson signed the Voting Rights Act of 1965, prohibiting most of the barriers that prevented African Americans from voting. The voting rights movement was not only for blacks. Other ethnic groups, especially Hispanics, also benefited as a result of their arduous struggle. Prodemocracy movements the world over looked to Alabama's African American voting rights movement as a source of inspiration and courage. Germans sang "We Shall Overcome," the voting rights movements' anthem, as they tore down the Berlin Wall in 1989. The same year, Chinese students in their movement for democratic reforms sang "We Shall Overcome" as they faced down government tanks in Beijing's Tiananmen Square. In 1994, the world joined the chorus with South Africans upon the dismantling of apartheid, electing Nelson Mandela president.

CHAPTER 14

The Civil Rights Act

THE CIVIL RIGHTS ACT of 1964 was a landmark piece of legislation that outlawed discrimination against blacks and women, including racial segregation. It ended unequal application of voter registration requirements and racial segregation in schools, at their workplace, and by facilities that serve the general public ("public accommodations"). Initially, the powers given to enforce the act were weak, but they were supplemented during later years.

The Voting Rights Act of 1965 outlawed discriminatory voting practices that had been responsible for the widespread disenfranchisement of African Americans in the United States. Echoing the language of the Fifteenth Amendment, the act prohibits states from imposing any voting qualification or prerequisite to voting, or standard practice, or procedure, to deny or abridge the right of any citizen of the United States to vote on account of race or color. Specifically, Congress intended the act to outlaw the practice of requiring otherwise qualified voters to pass a literacy test in order to register to vote, a principal means by which southern states have prevented African Americans from voting.

The act established extensive federal oversight of elections, providing that states with a history of discriminatory voting practices could not implement any change affecting voting without first obtaining the approval of the Department of Justice. These provisions applied to states (mostly in the South) that had used a device to limit voting and in which less than 50 percent of the population was registered to vote in 1964. The act was renewed and amended by Congress four times; a twenty-five-year extension was signed into law by President George W. Bush in 2006. The act is widely considered a landmark in civil rights legislation, though some of its provisions sparked political controversy. During the debate over the 2006 extension, some Republican members of Congress objected to renewing the preclearance requirements, arguing that it represented an overreach of federal power and placed unwarranted bureaucratic demands on southern states that have long since abandoned the discriminating practices the act was meant to eradicate. Conservative legislators also opposed requiring states with large Spanish-speaking populations to provide bilingual ballots. Congress nonetheless voted to extend the act for twenty-five years, with its original enforcement provisions left intact.

CHAPTER 15

I Remember

I REMEMBER GROWING UP in Atlanta. Life was wonderful for me and my family. I had a lovely childhood with two loving parents. My father worked two jobs as long as I could remember. I thought all fathers worked two jobs. My mother kept our home in order. Every weekend father took my brother and me to work with him, because Woolworth's was next door; they would discard damaged toys in their dumpsters, and we would retrieve the toys and bring them home. These toys were like new.

Our basement became like a toy warehouse. We were very popular in our neighborhood, because we gave away many of these toys, not knowing that we were doing charity work at a young age. We had every kind of toy that was made in this country, but yet we were very grounded and normal children. Our neighborhood was a normal place to live. Even though my father worked two jobs, he still found time to give us all of himself. He always believed in a loving home, and we were never without food. We always, and I mean always, had nice clothes to wear.

At night, our father worked at a parking lot. At eleven o'clock, he would close the lot, and at eight o'clock, he would walk across the street to his morning job at J. P. Allen.

In its heyday, this company was like one of today's best designer stores. During this time, only the well-to-do would shop there. This was one of the nation's top designer clothing stores. Our father was one of many delivery drivers; customers who shopped at J. P. Allen would have their purchases delivered to their homes. This was the only store in the city that offered this service.

The company truck was brown and gray, and the drivers' uniforms were pressed and starched. Every weekend when our father was making his routine deliveries, my older brother and I would ride along with him. Each and every stop we made, the families knew our father by name, as well as both of us. They were the friendliest, kindest, and most loving white people anyone could hope to meet. These were the movers and shakers of Atlanta. There were never any racist moments with them. Many times we would park the truck and sit down to eat lunch or dinner with them. Never, not one time, was anyone nasty toward us; not one.

Elsewhere in the city, however, there were problems. I remember the first time I rode on the back of a city bus (it was also the last time I would do so). On this day, my mother, brother, and I were going downtown. Instead of waiting on Father, Mother decided we should ride the bus. As we got on the bus, all of the seats in the front were empty. I was just a kid, seven years old, so I sat down in the first seat I came to. Mother then said to me that I could not sit there. We then walked past all those empty seats at the front of the bus to the back.

The bus continued on its route; at each stop, the driver would pick up riders, but something was very strange to me. At each stop, white people would get on, and they only sat in the seats at the front. When a black person got on the bus, they passed the empty seats at the front and walked to the back. The back of the bus was becoming overcrowded; soon, there was standing room only, right up to the middle of the bus.

Suddenly, at the next stop, the driver strangely enough did not stop for the people who were there waiting. He just drove right past them. I noticed these people were all black. As the driver continued to pass about three more stops with all black people, at the next stop he picked up only one person because this person was a white man. The driver told the other people (black) standing there alongside the one white man that there was no more room on the bus for them because all the space for black people was already full.

As the driver drove off leaving all of the remaining people behind, this rider had his choice of seats since there were at least enough empty ones for ten people and enough standing space for around fifteen more.

I asked mother why we as black people could not sit in the empty seats at the front of the bus. Just then we started hearing a loud car horn blaring behind the bus.

At first we didn't notice the car or the driver, but as the bus continued on its route there still was this horn getting louder and louder behind us until the bus driver stopped. The driver of the car blowing their horn walked around to the bus driver's side of the bus. I immediately saw and knew the person driving the car blowing their horn like a mad person; it was our father.

Father then told the bus driver from a standing position out in the middle of the street to stop this bus right then and there so that he could take his family off. Before the driver could answer my father, my mother, brother, and I exited the bus and walked with him back to his car. He then sternly remarked to us that as long as he has life in his body, his family would never ever again ride on the back of anyone's bus because of an unjust law. After a short period of time father bought two more cars, and we never again as his proud family, and true to his word, rode on a bus again. Mother explained to us later on that black people could not ride in the front of any buses, but only at the back because of Jim Crow laws which were made by white people.

When I entered my teen years, the rest of the country was having race riots between black and white people, but there was peace in Atlanta between the races. I am not saying all was peaceful between the races, but I did not hear of any trouble. We had jobs; we could shop at any stores we wanted to; we could eat anywhere we wanted to. Atlanta had so many strong black leaders; it was the cradle of the civil rights movement. Maybe this is why Atlanta was so calm while the rest of our country was going up in flames.

I went to David T. Howard High School, which was a few blocks away from the home of Daddy King. One day a friend and I cut class and left school. We were walking down Auburn Avenue, right by Daddy King's house, and just as we passed his house, Daddy King called out to us, "Why are you young men not in school? Why are you walking around this time of day?" I said the first thing that came to my mind: there was an emergency at home and we had to get there right away.

Just then Martin Jr. said, "Right, Father, do you remember how many times we have heard that one?"

Three weeks passed by and once again my friend and I left school early, but this time we made sure not to walk past Daddy King's house. But as fate would have it, we walked right past a church on Auburn Avenue, and as we were passing, Martin Jr. and his father came out of the church. Daddy King stared at us as though God himself was looking at us. Martin Jr. asked why we were not in school again, and then he told his father to go ahead to his meeting and he would take care of the two of us.

Suddenly fear took over my mind; I thought, *Oh, Lord, we are dead.* But Martin Jr. took us inside of the church and reprimanded us for about an hour. After he got his point across, we went back to school that same day and never again left school early. A year after our encounter with the Kings, I came to know who Daddy King and his son were; that church was Ebenezer Baptist Church. The memory that I have of them will be with me for the rest of my life. Thank you, Daddy King and Martin Luther King Jr., for saving me.

PARENTS TODAY

We are all in trouble. When you have empty heads raising empty heads, then society as a whole loses. When we as a community look around at our people, we see blacks committing violent acts against their own people and against all races in society; this is solid proof of a lack of learning and home training. We are not taking advantage of all this country has to offer us; we as a people, as black people, should help make our own situation better. We should ask ourselves where we went wrong. Why have we given up on ourselves, our children, and our country? So many lost souls are wandering the streets today. We have been set back thirty years, because from the 1980s through the 2000s, our communities have failed these young minds, which were left to develop by any means necessary other than their parents or the black community. The community of leaders, such as my parents, which were there for many decades, is all gone.

These leaders included Malcolm X, Daddy King, Dr. Martin Luther King Jr., Rep. John Lewis, former mayor Andy Young, former mayor Maynard Jackson, and Uncle Hosea Williams. When I was growing up, I knew that whenever I left our home, if I got into trouble or acted out in any way, my parents would find out and skin my butt raw. If Mrs. Mary on the corner found out that any child in her neighborhood was acting up anywhere, she would tear that butt up with her belt. Everybody knew about Mrs. Mary's belt; you did not want to face her, believe me on this. Our community was like Mrs. Mary's own personal military base. Black leaders were all around us, and they conducted themselves with a manner of respect and honor.

On any given day of the week, at Atlanta's Pascal's Restaurant on Hunter's Street, you might find many of the nation's civil rights leaders holding court. Many entertainers and politicians came in for good food and conversation. You would come in hungry and leave with not only your stomach full, but your soul and spirit full.

The Day That Changed the World

April 4, 1968, was the day that Dr. Martin Luther King Jr. was killed by an assassin's bullet. King was in Tennessee to help garbage collectors there, who were on strike. This reminded me again of the assassination of President Kennedy; here we go again. There was something wrong with our country. Somehow we healed from this horrible event and seemed to go on toward the future. Many singers were pumping out new songs; these soulful sounds were the rhythms of our people: James Brown's "Say It Loud, I'm Black and I'm Proud"; The Temptations' "Poppa Was a Rolling Stone"; Gladys Knight and the Pips; the Supremes; Aretha Franklin; and so many more that we connected with through the sounds of our daily lives.

Then came along the soulful sound of Marvin Gaye; even today, his songs still live on and guide us along our way. "What's Going On?" reaches into your soul. This was our people's way of dealing with day-to-day problems. We started going to movies to see people who looked like us in starring roles other than drug dealers, prostitutes, butlers, maids, or field hands. *Shaft, Cleopatra Jones, Sweet Sweet Back* were just a few movies in those days.

For the very first time in our history, we were more than slaves; we were people of importance, and the world had to give us respect. Even though they did not want to give us credit, our heads were held up high, shoulders back, backs straighter than ever before since we were bent from the weight of our past. From a kidnapped people, forced into slavery, raped, murdered, crippled under inhumane and egregious suffering, we now can walk upon this earth without the shackles of our past around our feet.

We finally have our own heroes and she-roes. Education is our way out of poverty. Nowadays a black man can support his family on his own sweat, standing strong in this world, having for the very first time in our history a chance to have a chance. I can only speak to you about my experiences. In most of our communities, we had modest houses and nice cars. We went to black schools. We shopped at the Curve Market, which was on Edgewood Avenue.

As a child, going to the Curve Market on a Saturday was better than going to Disneyland. Black, white, Chinese, and every nationality that lived in this city shopped at this market. Food, food, and more food was everywhere. You could just eat and eat until you could not walk. Funny, as I looked back on those times, people in the city got along with each other as one.

What happened to us? My father finally left Atlanta, and we moved away to Decatur. Our new home was truly a piece of America; new floors, painted walls, fenced in backyard, new roof, full basement, and an attic. We were surprised to have a white woman as our new neighbor, Mrs. Toy. Just like the theme song for the television show *The Jeffersons*, we were moving on up. Mrs. Toy welcomed us to our new neighborhood; she was one of the nicest persons I've ever met in my life.

There were three stores on the corner. There was a Jewish store, where you could buy food on credit during the week and then pay your account up on payday. Man, those two-for-one cookies were to die for. Right next door was Doc's Store, the neighborhood pharmacy. Doc's drugstore sold red hot smoke links for twenty-five cents. They were so good they made your eyes roll back in your head.

Across the street, Mr. Melvin had a store; believe it or not, he was a black man. In Decatur, we had the only block with this variety of entrepreneurs; a black, a Jew, and a white-owned store, and every one of them made money. We all got along and lived there about ten years. Not one person was robbed or locked up for stealing. This was not in our people's nature.

Every Saturday morning, the street was empty until noon, because cartoons were on TV. It was heaven in the city. Citywide, everyone was curled up with milk or orange juice, eating breakfast while watching

Mighty Mouse, Space Ghost, and *Looney Toons.* At the exact moment cartoons were over, you could look out on the streets and the children of Atlanta said, "Here we come."

In the downtown area, on one side of the street, Muslims sold their newspapers, and on the other side, the Black Panthers sold theirs; we all got along just fine together. Also downtown, they had the biggest and most glamorous movie theaters. There was the Lowe's Grand (which was where the premiere of *Gone with the Wind* was held), the Roxy, the Rialto, and the great Fox Theater. I remember black people could not enter through the main lobby entrance of the Fox Theater. We had to enter on the side of the building by walking up a towering flight of stairs on the outside.

We could only sit in the balcony. The balcony had the better seats, believe it or not, because you were closer to the ceiling, where there were millions of very small lights shining. When the main theater lights were turned down, you thought you were sitting up in heaven under the stars. Back in the day, almost every corner of downtown Atlanta had a stylish clothing store or fashionable shoe store. We had a few great ones: Out of Sight, Anthony's, Bvlgari, Dean Sample Shoes, Walton Hats, Robie Hats, Savil Shoes, Executive Shoes, and Friedman Shoes. Friedman carried large shoe sizes, and many famous athletes shopped there.

There was a whole floor that carried animal skin shoes: alligator, lizard, and ostrich boots. In the late summer evenings, you could cool down with silk shirts and pants, silk suits, pimp pants, as well as Bvlgari shirts for $300 a pop. There were mohair sweaters, silk pants, raw silk suits, shark skin suits, virgin wools, and belts matching your shoes and hats.

Growing up in Atlanta, there was an unspoken rule for black people: to remain safe, you had better keep your behind inside the expressway that surrounded the city. This was I-285. At that time, it was a three-lane highway that circled the city. Step outside of your safety zone, and you might have a very hard time with the racists living nearby. Here are some names of nearby cities surrounding Atlanta: Hapeville, Snellville, College Park, East Point, Riverdale, Conyers, Covington, and Marietta.

The sheriff of Douglas County was known for taking black prisoners out the back door of his jail and telling them he was letting them go.

Then as they left the building, he or his deputy would shoot them in the back, claiming they were trying to escape.

We now come to the land of the Ku Klux Klan. Stone Mountain has the largest granite rock in Georgia, and it was also the home base for this hate group. I remember once when the Klan came into our neighborhood and burned a cross. We pulled the ugly sight down and took the burned wood back to them and dumped it on their yard; yes, we knew where their yards were.

I knew Atlanta when she was a quiet town, but it has grown into the big city you see now. I remember once when the Klan obtained a permit to march through downtown on Marietta Street. At the time, the Omni Sports Arena had a large fence around the downtown complex. There were about fifteen Klansmen marching this day, and about ten state troopers guarding them, when from out of nowhere came about two hundred angry black men.

They stormed the fence around the Omni, and from their sheer weight, the fence collapsed. Before the fence hit the ground, the state troopers took off running down the street. The "tough" fifteen Klan members then took off running right behind the troopers. This was the funniest sight one could ever want to see.

The Klansmen were running so fast that some of them ran right out of their sheets, and others looked as though they were flying because their white sheets looked like capes, flying straight out in the wind. I will never forget that sight.

CHAPTER 16

Who Are We

FIRST WE WERE BROUGHT to this country as slaves. Then we were called Negroes, and later on, colored. During the seventies, we called ourselves black, and soon after, Afro Americans. Now we call ourselves African American. Do we really know who we are? Just think about this question. Our ancestors came from Africa, true enough, but we were born here in America; few of us have been to Africa. Some of us have never left the state we live in. This means we are Americans only. For centuries, our true nature has been hidden from us, and now we are hiding from our true nature.

Today's leaders are acting like they are on a reality TV show; public indecency has eroded our moral standing in this country. When there's a television show that has twenty-five beautiful women all pitting themselves against each other, to win one man by lying and twisting their own character, this is the wrong message to send our young daughters.

On another show, people eat worms, guts, butt parts, and eyeballs. They want to see who could outdo everyone else, no matter how horrible. Elsewhere, mothers often stand their children on the corner to ask for donations to help their schools raise money. This also is the wrong message: that they can beg for money out in the streets and people will give it to you. Gangster rappers are forming the minds of our young men. Rappers' only purpose is to sell garbage lyrics instead of real music to the already negative mind-sets. That is one of the main reasons we have lost thirty years of our young minds. After the death of Dr. Martin Luther King Jr., the soul of black people died with him.

Look at us black people. While Dr. King was alive we were strong; we were united in our voices; we stood strong in our community, not killing each other but showing respect toward each other. After Dr. King's death, we gained more freedom but grew further apart. Black-on-black crimes, especially involving our younger black males, have reached the point of no return. They have no respect for human life, for themselves, for each other.

They are antisocial, anti-community, and anti-country. We have lost three generations of young black males, and there is no saving them from themselves. They don't see their own destructive pathways; for example, they might go to prison or die. This is a group of people who don't feel that they need to be turned around. There is nothing anyone can say or do to save them. Those of you who are killing each other just because you can, you are now working for your enemy, the Klan.

The KKK no longer is needed to kill black people, especially black men. The mind-set of some black men is to kill each other behind something that makes no sense at all. As that old saying goes, the enemy of my enemy is my friend. Whenever there are two opposing sides in a war, and when one side can get the other side to turn on themselves, they become the other side's puppet; they are doing the work for their enemy. This becomes the perfect weapon.

Black men are killing each other and going to prison in very large numbers; this could only mean one thing. It becomes self-annihilation or genocide. If you are incarcerated, you can't raise a family. If you are deceased by the hands of another black male, thus doing the work of our enemy, they can now retire and just watch their perfect weapon at work.

I never would have thought I would live to witness some of these horrible acts. I am ashamed, embarrassed, saddened, and all I see is hopelessness on the faces of so many people, young and old. Some black people today have the attitude that society owes them something, just because they are black. Black-on-black crime, perpetuated by so many young black males, reinforces that they are only boys. These are not men, because the ones I grew up with were true men.

They fought and stood up for what was right and just; they worked and took care of their families, served their communities, and gave respect to others. But these young boys today are so full of BS that I must control my feelings as I write about them. We have lost three generations of minds; some of those who were born between the 1980s and 2000 (not all, and you know who I am speaking about) have no desire to improve themselves.

Before I go on any further, let me be clear: I do not give a damn about anyone getting angry or becoming upset at me for what I am about to say.

Bill Cosby, one of America's treasures, rose up through the school of hard knocks and made a life for himself and his family. I cannot speak for him, but I am sure he witnessed more injustice to our people than you and I combined. He lived to talk about it, taking the time out of his busy day and time away from his family. Yet he asked nothing from us but to just listen to what he, as a black man, a father, a person with a strong full past, experienced in this America. He reached out to us all so that we could try to come together as a nation, so that we would stop our young people from killing our sons or daughters, killing themselves, or killing us, so that we would help save our nation.

But most of you (and yes, you know who I am talking about) want to crucify Mr. Cosby because you did not like when he talked about you and your out-of-control, badass kids. Oh, by the way, these were the ones who were killing each other; remember them? They dropped out of school and run the streets day and night, breaking into our homes and raping our mothers, daughters, sisters, and wives. They have become a complete crime infestation in our community.

These are the ones who are walking around with their underwear showing. Whenever I see this, I just want to take a baseball bat and beat their butts. How disrespectful this is to the millions who came before us and fought and died; the millions who were slaves and did not have underwear to wear.

Today, rap music has such a powerful influence on our young people's minds; they should give a more uplifting, positive message: to be the best that we can be and encourage kids to stay in school and go onto higher education. Knowledge and unity is the only hope for us. Our fathers were real fathers, men being real men; rappers are sending the wrong message, telling our young kids to be the worst of mankind, being a roughneck, gangster, an outcast from society, a shot caller, a baller, the baldest n-word on the street.

They encourage them to make as many babies as they can and to have as many women as possible; this is what they call being a real player, yet they never say to support these babies or their mothers. Instead, they say to never let another black man punk you out because they looked at you, or accidentally stepped on your shoes, or because you did not like the color of his hat. Now nine-year-old boys, yes boys, are carrying big guns, just waiting to kill another black nine-year-old.

They call our beautiful women whores, or bitches, or my pussy. They tell you to beat her because you must keep your woman under control, show your boys you control your woman, because in their minds, this is how you treat a woman. On most rap videos, our beautiful young daughters are shown as pieces of meat, sex objects for any man to have, use, and then discard like an orange peel. These images are very negative to us all and the world, and especially to our younger people. Yet these rappers only care about their bottom line. Just think about the power these rappers would have over our young people and where would we all be if they used their music in a more positive way. We could change the whole world and take our rightful place.

We need more Bill Cosby's to take a strong stand against this self-inflicted violence. Most of us just turn our heads away from these problems because of our education or our status in the world; we just look down our noses and tell ourselves that this is not our problem; these are "those people's" problems. That's right, black people are calling other black people "those people."

SOME FACTS ACCORDING TO THE DEPARTMENT OF JUSTICE

More blacks in America are killed every year than the total number of US servicemen and women that have died in ten years of armed conflict in Iraq and Afghanistan.

In addition:

1. Blacks make up only 12.5 percent of the US population, yet they commit nearly 40 percent of the murders in America every year.

2. Nearly 50 percent of murder victims in America are black. Again, blacks make up only 12.5 percent of the total population.
3. Blacks kill more members of their own race every year than do all of the races in America, combined.

Let's take a timeout. Look at all of the big money rap stars, sports figures, movie stars, and entertainers earn. When they get those multimillion-dollar contracts, follow the money. When they go to buy those expensive cars, who do they buy them from? When they purchase multi-million dollar homes, who are the sellers? When they put diamonds and gold in their mouths, who sells it?

We can go on and on. So just in case your head is stuck up your rear end, all of those millions go right back to the people who gave it to them in the first place, the people who would not give a black person a cold glass of water on a very hot day. Once in a while, these big-money ballers might give away a turkey on Thanksgiving or some bikes and dolls, footballs, basketballs, and teddy bears, they then crawl back into their imaginary world and feel that they have done something important.

Well, let's look again at our world in America. Count all of the products in every store in this country. Choose any grocery store, and you will find there are thousands of items, multiple companies selling their products and services. How many of these companies are owned by black people? There are many car companies, and we buy millions of cars, spending trillions of dollars. Are any car companies owned by black people? Do we own the grocery stores where we get our food? Do we own any pharmacies? Look around you. Money is lying all around us, on the ground and on every street sign, stop sign, traffic light, and street light; on every road we drive and every building we walk past. These materials represent manufacturing monies that someone utilized to mass produce and then sold.

Our country has millions of buildings, but how many of them are owned by black people? Many people are here from all around the world; they were not even born here but they own their own businesses: Dairy Queen, Subway, and Dunkin Donuts. Black hair products in this country are a $9 billion industry, and yet the Koreans dominate this industry by selling the products to black people. Most of them could not speak English, so how do they get permits, build the buildings, and do their finances? It makes you wonder what is wrong with these pictures of success; why don't we achieve the same or more, given we are natural citizens?

I am not saying that people from other countries should not own their own business. They are united together as a people. Their families are encouraged to have their very own business, elevating their status by being in control of their own future, depending only on themselves.

As black people, having been born here, we survived our struggle for civil rights and human rights; we are natural citizens of this country, fighting and dying every day. We owe the millions of black people who have made sacrifices to enable people from around the world to be here and own their own businesses and homes. We need our butt kicked because as black people, we work so hard against each other, and this is one reason we are not successful: we do not work together.

Here during the late summer music festival in midtown (a three day event), over three hundred thousand people come together, mostly Whites, and not one shot is heard, not one argument or fight, but just people enjoying the weekend.

Sad to say, but put three black males on any corner, any city, and somebody has to argue, fight, shoot, or cut someone, usually about something trivial. We just have to turn the party out, have to be seen or heard, or loudly exclaim, "I got mines." What is wrong with us as a people?

I notice in the construction business when Hispanics drive to work, there are about twenty of them in one vehicle. When they take lunch, they eat together like a family. They work together and never, never fight or argue. When the day is over, they all pile back in their cars and trucks and drive home together. Imagine now three black males in three separate cars; they are usually late and never come back from lunch on time; most of them have problems at work because first, they don't want to be there, and second, they only want to work when they want to. The Hispanics come to this country with one car, and about six months later, they are all driving nice vehicles and working in their own businesses.

Now let us look at those three brothers (if they are still working and not dead or locked up). They are still working on someone else's job and driving a car that is twenty years old. Their car might cost $500, but they will spend $6,000 on rims, tires, and tinted windows, trying to "blackenize" it, because they want to look good riding around town. We still spend most of our lives being worker bees and simple consumers; we are still waiting on the return of the Lord to save us, so that we can return back home to live in paradise. Then why do you suppose God made this world and put us here?

What has happened to us today? We have the first black president and yet have lost our way. When we lived under the Jim Crow laws, there were no civil rights or voter's rights; we did not have any so-called rights, but as black people, we were stronger and lived as one people. We invented more and created more. Could someone give me an answer to this question: What is different now? Is something wrong with us as a people? Where did we lose our way? Just how desperate are people around the world to come here? We, as black Americans, are born here; all we have to do today is open our eyes and apply ourselves. Sadly, the majority of us are still waiting for the sky to open up and make everything perfect. The next section speaks for itself.

X-RAY OF TRAILER TRUCK

Migrants from Latin America and Asia were caught inside an eighteen wheeler trailer truck, after being detected by police X-ray equipment. Two trailer trucks heading to the U. S. and containing about 513 migrants were discovered at a checkpoint on early Tuesday, May 17. Sadly, there were no ventilation or restroom facilities inside the vehicle and yet they were willing to risk their lives just to get to this wonderful country of ours.

(Research the Reuters photo of the immigrants
inside the truck from May 18, 2011)

CHAPTER 17

Inventory

BLACK AMERICANS SPEND ABOUT $1 Trillion per year. So this only leaves us to be in a class of worker bees and consumers. We are under the principle of "ricochet money." This means the moment we get paid and our money hits our hands, it then ricochets right back into the hands of the people who control our lives. These are the people who are very wealthy simply because of us, the consumers. We as black people make nothing or own nothing; yes, there are a few owners, but it is a very, very small number.

Next, take any church on a normal Sunday. If membership is five thousand people, and if everyone gave a dollar every Sunday toward a business fund, at the end of every year, you would have about $240,000. The members could start up a new business and hire their own people, taking control of their lives.

Take pro athletes. They could take one third of their salary and start up their own business. Each year as their business grows, they could hire more and more of our own people, and thus we will be able to make some of the money from that $1 trillion that we spend. We have the power to lift our people up from their backs, to educate them, and grow our own businesses.

HERE IN ATLANTA

Recently, the Atlanta Housing Authority accepted applications to get on a waiting list for free housing. This was just a waiting list, but remember, a bird in the hand is better than two in a bush. If you went to get an application and saw there were already five hundred people ahead of you for just sixty slots, you might turn and walk away. But thirty thousand people showed up, and as we all know, that many black people showing up for something free could be a catastrophe.

You might think that this was a very sad day for black people, because the whole world was watching us, and you know anytime one black person gets caught up in something bad, then all black people are judged together as one. Hard to believe, but one woman was interviewed and said she had been waiting for eighteen years just to get public housing assistance. My God, she could have earned a doctorate degree, and become a heart surgeon or lawyer in that time. She could have started her very own business, or bought her family the greatest home that money could buy, during all those wasted years.

But she didn't. She was waiting for something free. This sounds similar to most churchgoing people: "I am just waiting on the Lord because he promised me." Well, the Lord has given us everything and then more. The Lord is waiting on you to get up and get going. The Lord is omnipresent. Guess who the Lord is waiting on? You.

After every big holiday, we usually only talk about how much food we ate or how drunk we got: "Man, I ate so much food I couldn't walk; I ate like a pig; man, we got so drunk." Imagine this conversation and how it must sound to an outsider. How many people are hungry in the world? Did you share that food with anyone? Turn the page and flip the script.

Now imagine how the conversation went with the people who sold all the food and drinks, beer, and liquor we just consumed. Just in case you hadn't thought about it, their conversation was with their bankers, telling them how much money they just made from their holiday sales. They made sure their family finances were in order so they could stay in control of their lives.

Come back to us now, and remember our foolish conversations. What is the difference between us and them? Taking the two scenarios into consideration, which group do you want to be a part of? It's your choice after all.

CHAPTER 18

Bad Influence: Demagogue

A WORD CAN BE more powerful than any weapon known to man. Today, with so many avenues for information, the wrong message can reach the minds of our young people. These daily influences are taking over their minds. There are pocket-sized computers and smart phones; the average US home has at least two televisions with twenty-four hours of news from around the world; information is constantly bombarding us from every country and every subject people can talk about. YouTube, Facebook, Twitter, MySpace, and other social media outlets are influencing the minds of our young people.

MTV, BET, RAPCITY, and other cable channels are shown around the world. So the only way we can save our children from these daily influences is to monitor them; this is not only impossible, impractical, and immoral, it would also stop their personal growth.

Our children listen to rap stars with names such as Scarface, Ghost Rider, Young Killer, Murder Inc., Bad Boy, Young Thug, and Al Capone.

There are so many other rappers who carry very dangerous and negative images to our young people. Just listen to their lyrics and watch their videos.

You can draw your own conclusions about the messages being sent out. So many of our young people use these videos as role models in their lives, so they figure they only have to imitate the very negative influences on the videos to be cool. They place tattoos all over their bodies, wherever there is skin available. Others wear dreadlocks or droopy pants. No business in their right mind will hire these kids, because their first impression of them is very negative and this image is bad, bad news for a prospective employer.

So now, because no one will hire our young people, they turn to crime; and thus turn on their own people. Since they have no jobs, what is left for them to do? A life of crime awaits our young people, and that is only if they do not get killed first. If a life of crime does not kill them, then prison awaits. After incarceration for many years, some are released right back into society, meaner, with less education, further behind the eight ball, with no jobs and no other means of support. So guess what happens next? They go right back into a life of crime. This sad, vicious circle is all they understand.

CITIZENSHIP LOST

The most important part of being born in the United States is to have the most prestigious citizenship in the world. So many people of every race have fought and died for us all to have this wonderful gift. We were born here, so our citizenship is automatic. Yet freedom must be earned, and we must fight to protect our citizenship.

THE CONSTITUTION OF THE UNITED STATES, AMENDMENT 14: CITIZENS' RIGHTS (1868)

SECTION I. ANY PERSON born or naturalized in the United States and governed by it is a citizen of the United States and of the state in which he resides. No state can make laws that abridge any right, privilege, or protection of citizens of the United States; nor pass laws that may cost a person his life, imprison him, or fine him, unless he has been found guilty of a crime in a court of law by due process of law. No state may deny any person, under its government, equal protection of the law.

Amendment 15: Voting Rights of African Americans (1870)
Section 1. The rights of citizens of the United States to vote cannot be taken away because of a person's race, color, or previous condition of servitude. Keeping and knowing all of the rights of citizenship will determine how far you go in life. It is solely up to you. No one can deny where you are allowed to live or what business you might want to

own. We now have a black president of the United States of America. Never again can the excuse be used that the white man is keeping black people down.

The only person holding you back is you. But it will take hard work. Anything worth having is worth fighting for. The main point of this chapter is to encourage you to protect all of your rights as a citizen of the United States. Do not let your family, friends, boys, girls, lovers, or yourself give away your freedom by committing crimes that will put you in trouble with the law.

As long as you may live, this country's system is the best in the world, so use the laws to work for you, not against you. When we realize this system can work for us, then we can be truly free. Think of all the people before us who were denied their freedom; it is up to us to make sure they did not die in vain. Their sacrifices were for our freedom and for the future freedom for our people.

IGNORANT ASS NEGROES

I have no problem about race mixing; I feel that people have the right to date and marry whomever they want to. My problem is when I hear black men saying that they only date white women and would never date a black woman. This is a very ignorant ass Negro. If white women are your cup of tea, fine, go for them. But can anyone tell me why these men feel the need to tell the world that a black woman is not good enough for them?

I cannot ever recall hearing a white man say that he'd rather only date black women. If white women are what you want in your life, then keep your ignorance to yourself and just do your thing.

Black women have had enough prejudices and setbacks from the world; they surely don't need black men to keep kicking them down; sad. These ignorant ass Negroes are putting down their own mothers, sisters, and grandmothers, because it was a black woman who carried their ignorant ass, who gave them life, who raised them to become the men they are today. So rather than being respectful, they come along as an ignorant ass Negro.

Black women: oh my God, thank you for making me a black man. This choice is easy for me, knowing what I know now about the beautiful blackness of the black woman. But God has already made this choice for me, and I give thanks. A black woman understands my pain as a black man. A black woman has walked alongside me through my plight of racism, hatred, injustice, disrespect, and unfairness in this country. She alone knows of our people's suffering. Her eyes calm me when I am angry.

I may have the weight of the world on my shoulders, but the moment I look into her eyes, they tell me that all is right again with all of the unconditional love within them. You can place a black woman on any stage alongside ten other women, from every other race in the world, and she would have more class, more presence, and more stature. Her beauty will stand alone.

There are many beautiful women in every race around the world. There's only one woman in this world for me to love, and she is my black queen. Many people call black women angry, but this is because of their ignorance. Black women are very strong. Their strength is misunderstood as anger; it can be hard to get along with. Black women have been carrying the black race from slavery up until today.

The weakest link in the black family is the black man. They are missing in action, not there for their family, not strong men, not standing in for injustice, not good fathers, and not good husbands; they leave home, never to return. Some are killed by the hatred in this country; others are killed by other black men. Yet through it all, a black woman rises every day, carrying the weight of her people on her shoulders, raising her children alone, going to work and keeping the family together, against all odds.

She still carries on by herself. Could you walk in her shoes while keeping a smile on your face? I will answer this one for you. Sadly, many people criticize her for being angry, especially her very own black male counterparts. Most black women are strong. This is just who they are; sometimes, they grew up in harsh conditions. This hardened them even more, so when black men say they don't date black women, they really are saying they cannot deal with a strong woman in their lives.

This is because they are very weak men; they are looking for a woman they can easily control and have their way with. The main reason for their insecurity is they are still little boys inside. They want to pretend to be players so they can run around and have multiple relationships with as many women as they can. They then have the nerve to come and go from home as they please, and the women in their lives are expected to say nothing about these sorry actions. As we all know, a strong black woman will not stand for that whorish attitude.

A strong black woman would leave him or make him leave; better than that, she will put a beat down on his ass and then put his ass out. We all know the truth as to why black women are getting a bad rap.

CORE PRINCIPLES

Having core principles in one's life is essential; here are my own principles:

1. I love my wife.
2. I love my family.
3. There are some things that I will not do, no matter what the price.
4. I will never violate my values.
5. I will not let someone talk me into doing something against my will.
6. If I feel that something's wrong, then count me out.
7. I am a citizen of the United States of America, meaning I will follow the laws of my country.
8. I love my country.
9. I respect the differences of others.
10. Responsibility, obligation, and commitment all command respect.
11. I will do my best to become the best that I can become.
12. I will strive to be honest at all times.

I will take these attributes to my grave. A person of good conscience will have principles, morals, and values in their lives. They will also teach their children these qualities so they too will be given a great chance at life.

STACKED DECK AGAINST US

Today, we as black people are faced with many enemies. They are all around us. They are in our own family, our communities, our schools, our jobs, our churches. The leaders of the pack can be found in their beautiful skyscrapers or on the golf courses of America.

They are up bright and early, reshaping, twisting, and changing the laws of this country, making sure that the rules of the game favor only them and no one else. They make sure that they put their own judges and politicians into positions of power. Whenever one of their family members is in trouble, all they have to do is make a phone call. Their troubles mysteriously disappear, and all is well once again for them.

We all know who I am talking about. They can call their friends at the bank and get another loan, even though they haven't paid back the last ten loans they took out. In other words, because white America controls all of the wealth in this country, we are at their mercy and under their control. Yes, I said control.

Today, they could pull black people out of their homes and kill them in the streets; they don't, but not because they are afraid of the law; remember that they make the laws. They know that killing black people would start a race war, and they would lose their own loved ones. They also know we would win this war and then be in charge of the country. So they must attack us by any means necessary, without firing a shot.

This keeps us under their control; they have all the wealth, and the deck is stacked against us. By changing laws and keeping antiquated ones on the books, they make damn sure they keep the right people in power so the laws favor them. This is how white America keeps control.

REDLINING

This means raising the prices on housing so that only the well-to-do can afford them; they are also able to attend the best schools, where only a select few are accepted (or can even afford).

The price of houses in certain neighborhoods is enormous; cars at certain dealership are overpriced; and prices at some restaurants are so high that normal people can't afford them. These are just a few ways that black people are redlined. This is just another weapon that our enemies use against us.

Redistricting

This process divides up districts in order to change congressional representation. This means keeping control of the state and federal government. This also controls what laws are approved; once again, another level of control over our lives. Yes, these weapons are also used against a lot of poor white people too. Poor people, sad to say, are also casualties of this war.

The new KKK is composed of people with power in large companies. They are in Congress and are consumed with hatred against anyone who is different from themselves.

These people have hung up their hoods and white sheets and turned them in for black and grey suits with ties, holding powerful political positions.

But for experienced persons of color, we look at these people and can see the obvious hatred in their eyes, hear it in their voices, and see it in their actions; most of them still have cotton residue around their mouths, even though they pulled the white hoods and sheets from their bodies. The traces of their ignorant hatred are regrettably still there.

Chapter 19

Lost Gospels

ABOUT THIRTY YEARS AGO, I first heard that there were approximately twenty-seven lost gospels. A few months later, I heard that only eleven lost gospels existed, and finally, someone said there were only four lost gospels.

For those of you who don't understand the meaning of the lost gospels, several parts of the Holy Bible are missing. There were people who decided what books were to remain in the Holy Bible and what were to be left out. You might ask yourself why anyone would go to all this trouble.

Strangely enough, four of the missing gospels fell into my arms. As I began reading these gospels, my eyes opened up, and for the very first time, I had a clear understanding about religion.

My purpose for speaking about these lost gospels; is so you have information about them for yourselves. We can make up our own minds about what the world should or should not know. But it is wrong for a select few to decide for us all.

CONSTANTINE I: 57 EMPEROR OF THE ROMAN EMPIRE

Christianity was started about 300 AD, by a group of Jews who followed the teaching of Jesus. The story of Jesus was first written down in the Gospel of Mark, in 70, about forty years after the death of Jesus.

By the year 200, there were about fifty gospels, including the Gospel of Phillip, Gospel of Hebrews, and the Revelation of Peter.

The Christian Bible as we know it did not appear until about 300 years after Jesus.

In 312, a Roman emperor named Constantine, a pagan who believed in multiple gods, claimed to have had a vision of a cross before a battle. After his victory, he converted to Christianity.

In 325, Emperor Constantine convened the Council of Nicaea; he summoned the most powerful priests and bishops from around the world to decide the basic tenets of Christianity. After a long meeting, they all agreed on seven principles that unified all of Christianity.

Control of the religion was placed under the emperor. Constantine decided on which books were to be included in the Bible and which were to be left out. He only allowed the gospels of Matthew, Mark, John, and Luke. What happened to the other gospels? In 382, the church considered all other gospels heresy and banned them.

Constantine also made new laws regarding the Jews. They were forbidden to own Christian slaves or to circumcise their slaves. The priests and bishops then went around telling the people what they should or should not read. What was in those banned gospels? Why didn't they want the people to read them?

No one knew nearly two thousand years ago that the Gospel of Peter would emerge in 1886 from the sands of the Egyptian desert; other gospels were discovered in the twentieth century. There was the Gospel of Thomas, the Gospel of Mary Magdalene, and the Gospel of Judith. These lost gospels revealed a different view of Jesus and a different approach to spirituality. This lost version of Christianity threatened the very foundation of the faith itself.

For nearly two thousand years, Christians believed that there were only four gospels that told the story of Jesus of Nazareth. When the Gospel of Peter was discovered, it suggested a secret history of forbidden scribes.

In 1945, a remarkable discovery was made that changed the history of Christianity forever: a farmer in Egypt found a sealed clay jar with an 1,800-year-old payload: fifty-two separate gospels, with titles like the Acts of Peter and the Apostolic of James.

The Gospel of Thomas contained the sayings of Jesus. It repeated many of the things found in the New Testament. The Gospel of Thomas was agnostic.

Agnostics were a sect of early Christianity that had a deep emphasis on mysticism; they disagreed with many of the church's higher teachings.

Agnosticism was saved by secret knowledge. They were true followers of Jesus if you understood this secret knowledge. They believed that true humanity is within oneself and that the peace of God is within. Why would anyone need a priest or bishop? In the Gospel of Thomas, Jesus conveyed a strange and secret message, a teaching that was very different from the traditional gospel teachings.

The traditional teaching is that Jesus is the only son of God. The Gospel of Thomas taught that we all can become the sons and daughters of God. It said that when you know yourself, you will understand that you are all children of the living father.

"Agnostic" means "one who knows"; *gnostic* is a Greek word meaning knowledge. The Gospel of Thomas calls for a personal connection with God, without the need for organized churches, priest, or bishops. The Gospel of Thomas is older than the Gospels of Mark, Matthew, Luke, and John. The Gospel of Thomas only contains the sayings of Jesus, whereas the other gospels describe the miracles and stories of Jesus.

For centuries, Christians believed that there were only four gospels. In 1896, another gospel appeared in Egypt, with a very surprising author: Mary Magdalene. She was one of Jesus' disciples and a member of his inner circle. Women were once powerful leaders in the Christian church. Mary Magdalene was not (as the infamous lie says) a reformed prostitute; she was a leader of the apostles.

The most important gospel was written by a woman. The Gospel of Mary details the secret instructions that Jesus gave only to Mary about life, death, and heaven. Jesus described the afterlife to Mary in agnostic terms. The afterlife described in the four gospels tells of a blissful paradise, but the Gospel of Mary describes a strange journey of the soul after death; people encounter angelic and demonic beings as the soul makes it way to heaven.

It was only to Mary that Jesus revealed this journey of the soul to heaven. The gospel reported that Peter, the leader of the apostles, became very angry after hearing about Mary.

Peter said, "Did he really speak to a woman without our knowledge? Are we to turn about and listen to her? Why did he prefer her to us?"

In the gospel, the apostles overrode Peter's denouncing of Mary and supported her, saying if the savior made her, then who were we to reject her? Mary understood the mind of Jesus; there was a spiritual connection or bond between them, and she could motivate people. Mary was thought to be a person of insight, a leader.

The Gospel of Mary gave a different view as to what the message of Jesus was; Mary Magdalene understood that point of view in ways that the other disciples did not. This gospel, which was written in 200 AD, revealed that there was a struggle in the early church about the role of women.

In 1886, French archaeologists working in Egypt uncovered an ancient tomb. In it was a treasure: an eighth-century monk clutching his hands around a book—the Gospel of Peter. This lost gospels told a different story of Jesus.

One of the most recent gospels found was uncovered in 2006: the lost Gospel of Judith in Nag-Hammadi, Egypt. In the Gospel of Judith, Jesus recognized that Judith was the wisest of the apostles. Judith was thought to be a very special apostle. He received enlightenment and was most insightful about who Jesus really was. Jesus said Judith would only deliver his physical body to the Romans. He therefore would escape crucifixion and return to the spiritual realm. They believed that we could get rid of this human body and return to the actual spiritual existence of our true selves. This occurred sometime between 280 and 330, almost three hundred years after the death of Jesus.

Our people are so easy to be led under other people's leadership. All I am asking you is not to just accept what someone else is telling you as the truth. Please, do your homework, check and double check your findings, because the truth is running away from you. So many of us will not do the hard work, because it is so easy to allow others to do it for us and then bring their findings to us. What I do know is whatever you give energy to becomes your reality.

Your thoughts and beliefs become your chosen path on your journey. Giving your energy to a demonic being only brings into existence to this devil. He becomes real in your life out of fear. Then fear controls your life; just fear. Hell is of others' making. If we know that we all are children of a living father, then fear should never be part of our lives, because our father is within us all.

Scholars of the lost gospels include Robert R. Cargill, archeologist of UCLA (the Gospel of Thomas); Marvin Meyer, Chapman University; S. Scott Bartchy, professor of Christian history UCLA; and Darrell L. Bock, Dallas Theological Seminary.

CHAPTER 20

The Disrespect of America's First Black President and Double Standards

DURING PRESIDENT OBAMA'S RUN for office, Michelle Obama was quoted as saying, "For the very first time in my life, I am proud of my country." Half of white America cried out to condemn her for this comment.

Two years later, Michele Bachmann, during her run for president, made almost the same statement; she said that she had regained her respect for her country. Not one word was said against her. Now what is the difference between the two statements? Both have the same meaning. The only difference is that one woman is black and the other is white.

DOUBLE STANDARDS

They wanted to nail Michelle Obama's feet to the cross, but Michele Bachmann got a free pass and continued on as if nothing she said was wrong. Even today, parts of this country continue to show their disrespect toward black people.

Most of the GOP and the Tea Party, as well as the powers to be in this country, continue to prove that racism and hatred is alive and well. Do not be fooled by their red, white, and blue Christian signs. Thanks to President Obama, it has been brought out in the open again; this evil spirit of racist hatred is still alive today in this country. It doesn't matter if it destroys innocent people, regardless of their color, just so that it destroys President Obama by making him fail as president.

Even the big banks that the president gave billions of dollars to save from going under are holding on to enormous sums of money so that the economy will continue to drop and unemployment will continue to climb. Some corporations are also holding on to money that would definitely help create jobs. Republican governors, congressmen and congresswomen, and senators have one main goal: to destroy President Obama; so what if the rest of the country is going to hell and people are dying from not having health care?

Recently, a young black father died from a tooth infection because he had no health insurance. Just think what might have been if only he had assistance from the richest country in the world, his country of birth; he would be alive today, and there's no telling what miracles he could have given to the world. Millions of people are losing their homes, and families are being put out on the street. White people, black people, and all races are being affected by this criminal hatred.

While President Obama was speaking to Congress, a congressman from South Carolina yelled out in a loud and disrespectful voice, saying, "You lie." Never before in this country's history have people displayed so much disrespect for the office of the presidency. This disrespect continues on and on. But why is it only coming from white people?

Most Republicans have displayed so much disrespect to President Obama, calling him such horrible names as coonskin, monkey, ape, and liar. Senator Mitch McConnell of Kentucky said his first priority was to make President Obama a one term president. Senator Kyl of Arizona made a speech about Planned Parenthood. He stated that 90 percent of the money that goes to Planned Parenthood was being used for abortions. After making this statement in front of Congress and the American people, knowing all along it was a lie, he caught heat from Planned Parenthood and retracted his statement, saying he had misspoken. He claimed he was just giving his opinion and did not truly mean the words that came out of his mouth. This was just another white Senator with lies in his heart, and I have just gotten started.

"BIRTHERS"

Many Republicans and Tea Party members went around the country claiming that President Obama was not born in America, all the while knowing this was truly the biggest lie ever. Before anyone can become president of the United States, their background is closely checked by government agencies. To stain President Obama, though, they kept up with this horrible lie, which in turn caused the world to criticize America for trying to destroy their very own president. Congressman Joe Walsh of Illinois went on YouTube and said this: "President Obama, you need to stop lying about the debt ceiling, that if we do not raise the debt ceiling what could happen to America's credit rating." Joe Walsh lied and nothing happened. But after all the lies the GOP and the Tea Party told, our country's credit rating was lowered for the very first time in our history. Not one GOP or Tea Party member said that President Obama was correct and they were damned wrong.

While President Bush was in office for eight years and the GOP held both houses, they raised the debt ceiling eight times without any hesitation. They also put us into two illegal wars, which took us from a budget surplus to $4 trillion in debt. This was just fine when President Bush did it, because he was a white man. Now, white folks are mad.

After eight years of the Bush-Cheney disaster, now you get mad? You did not get mad when the Supreme Court stopped a legal recount of Bush's ballots and appointed him president.

You did not get mad when Cheney allowed energy company officials to dictate energy policy and push us to invade Iraq.

You did not get mad when Cheney blew the cover of a covert CIA operative.

You did not get mad when the Patriot Act got passed.

You did not get mad when we illegally invaded a country that posed no threat to us.

You did not get mad when we spent over $800 billion (and counting) on illegal wars. You did not get mad when Bush borrowed more money from foreign sources than the previous forty-two presidents combined.

You did not get mad when $10 million of Saddam Hussein's cash just disappeared in Iraq; now it is up to $60 billion, gone.

You did not get mad when you found that we were torturing people.

You did not get mad when Bush embraced trade and outsourcing policies that shipped six million American jobs out of this country.

You did not get mad when the government was illegally wiretapping Americans.

You did not get mad when we did not catch Osama bin Laden.

You did not get mad when President Bush rang up $10 trillion in combined budget and current account deficits.

You did not get mad when you saw horrible conditions in Walter Reed Hospital.

You did not get mad when we let a major US city, New Orleans, drown after Hurricane Katrina.

You did not get mad when we gave people who have more money than they could spend, the filthy rich, over $1 trillion in tax breaks.

You did not get mad when we had the worst eight years of no job creation under Bush.

You did not get mad when over two hundred thousand US citizens lost their lives because they had no health insurance.

You did not get mad when a lack of oversight by the Bush administration caused citizens to lose $12 trillion in investments, retirement, and home values.

You finally got mad when a black man was elected president and decided that people in America had the right to see a doctor if they were sick; yes, illegal wars, lies, corruption, torture, job losses by the millions, stealing your tax dollars to make the rich richer, and the worst economic disaster since 1929 are all okay with you, but helping fellow Americans who are sick? "Oh, hell no."

At a 2011 Republican debate, Governor Rick Perry was asked if he lost any sleep over the 234 people who were executed on his watch, and before he could answer, the audience started to applaud very loudly, approving the executions.

In another Republican debate in Florida, Tea Party Congressman Ron Paul, who happens to be a doctor, was asked what we should we do if a thirty-year-old man who did not have health insurance had to be hospitalized and slipped into a coma. Before Congressman Paul gave his answer, several people shouted out loudly, "Let him die!"

Not one Republican leader denounced these horrible responses. These are the people who are now in the GOP. They act like domestic terrorists. During President Obama's first four years in office, the Republicans said no to any and all proposals he has offered to help the country.

When will people come together to put country first rather than permitting this small group of racist people to make choices for all of us? If we stand silent and keep quiet, knowing that these people are wrong, then we are just as guilty as them.

Here's another example of the GOP in action involving Carl Lewis, another great black American.

CARL LEWIS

Nationality: United States African American
Born 07/01/1961
Birmingham, Alabama
Residence: Medford, New Jersey
Competitor for the United States Olympic games
Medals won:
    Gold - 1984 Los Angeles 100 m
    Gold – 1984 Los Angeles 200 m
    Gold – 1984 Los Angeles 4 x 100 m relay
    Gold – 1984 Los Angeles long Jump
    Gold – 1988 Seoul long Jump
    Gold -- 1992 Barcelona 4 X 100 m relay
    Gold - 1992 Barcelona long jump
    Gold – 1996 Atlanta long jump
    Silver – 1988 Seoul 200 m
World Championships:
    Gold – 1983 Helsinki 10 m
    Gold – 1983 Helsinki 4 X 100 m relay
    Gold – 1983 Helsinki long jump
    Gold – 1987 Rome 100 m
    Gold – 1987 Rome 4 X 100 m relay
    Gold – 1987 Rome long jump
    Gold – 1991 Tokyo 100 m
    Gold – 1991 Tokyo 4 x 100 m relay
    Silver – 1991 Tokyo long jump
    Bronze – 1993 Stuttgart 200 m

Pan American Games
Gold – 1987 Indianapolis long jump
Gold – 1987 Indianapolis 4 x 100 m relay
Bronze – 1979 San Juan long jump

Lewis was a dominant sprinter and long jumper who topped the world ranking in the 100 m, 200 m, and long jump event's frequently from 1981 to the early 1995. He was named athlete of the year by track and field news in 1982, 1983, and 1984, and set world records in the 100 m, 4 x 100 m and 4X 200 m relays. His world record in the indoor long jump has stood since 1984 and his 65 consecutive victories in the long jump achieved over a span of 10 years is one of the sports longest undefeated streaks.

His lifetime accomplishments have led to numerous accolades, including being voted "Sportsman of the century" by the international Olympic Committee and being named "Olympian of the century" by the American sports magazine Sports Illustrated. He also helped transform track and field from its nominal amateur status to its current professional status, thus enabling athletes to have more lucrative and longer lasting careers.

GOP Lawmaker Quits over Wife's E-Mail to Carl Lewis

In Trenton, New Jersey, a freshman Republican lawmaker resigned because his wife sent an offensive and racist e-mail to the Democratic state senate campaign office of nine-time Olympic gold medalist Carl Lewis. Jennifer Delaney's e-mail said, in part, "Imagine having dark skin and name recognition and the nerve to think that equaled him knowing something about politics." Pat Delaney decided to leave office to shield his three children from a "hurtful and embarrassing public spectacle involving their mother."

Delaney's wife inexplicably sent and offensive and racist e-mail in response to a routine e-mail from Carl Lewis' campaign; Jennifer Delaney's racist e-mail was inexcusable. Delaney said in a statement that he and his wife did not share the same racial views. He said he was sorry "on behalf of my family, and we sincerely apologize to Mr. Lewis for any pain this has caused him."

In 1936, Jessie Owens faced Hitler and Germany at the Olympics, on top of the racial hatred from his own country. Like Carl Lewis and President Obama, he stayed fast to his heart for his country.

Here are President Obama, Carl Lewis, and Jessie Owens; three different men in three different time periods. President Obama, America's first black president, put himself through school and graduated first in his class. He became a US Senator and abided by all the laws of this country, his country. He also won the Nobel Peace Prize. Carl Lewis is a world-class athlete and Olympic champion, and Jessie Owens also won Olympic gold medals. Jessie Owens also won Olympic gold medals.

But this evil spirit of racial hatred in America today has been around from our very beginning. It will destroy our moral fabric because of the ignorance of the few. When we witness this racial hatred and stand silent, turn our heads, then we are allowing this evil to grow and fester. We also become a part of this evil, because we did nothing to eradicate it.

If you do not stand against this monstrous evil, look in the mirror, because it is really you.

NO RESPECT, NO JUSTICE, NO FAIRNESS

Jesse Owens's inclusion on the US Olympic team was controversial, because it came at a time when segregation and discrimination against black people was normal in much of the United States. In Berlin, Owens was able to freely use public transportation and enter bars and other public facilities without the difficulty he would face as a black man in the United States.

When it was reported that Hitler had refused to shake his hand after his victories, Owens said "When I passed the chancellor he arose and waved to his man of the hour in Germany." He also stated Hitler did not snub him, but FDR did. The president did not even send him a telegram.

Hitler did, however, leave Olympic Stadium just before another African American athlete, Cornelius Johnson, was set to receive his medal. The German victories obviously made him happy, but he was highly annoyed by Owens's series of triumphs. People whose ancestors came from the jungle were primitive, Hitler said with a shrug; their physiques were stronger than those of civilized whites and hence should be excluded from future games.

German crowds adored Owens, and he forged a long term friendship with a German competitor, Luz Long.

No justice. No respect. No fairness. All we ask is respect, justice, and fairness.

According to a 2011 story in the *Daily Caller,* an online news publication, Republican Senators John McCain of Arizona and Lindsey Graham of South Carolina praised the end of Muammar Gaddafi's forty-year reign in Libya but criticized America's limited use of airpower in the fight to overthrow him. "Americans can be proud of the role our country has played in helping to defeat Gaddafi, but we regret that this success was so long in coming due to failure of the United States to employ the full weight of our airpower," the two senators said in a joint statement, after praising the Libyan rebels who drove Gaddafi from out of nowhere.

Graham and McCain also called on the United States to lead the international community and provide the support that Libyans need in the post-Gaddafi era. Graham and McCain said US involvement will be determined by how fair the government that replaces Gaddafi's regime turns out to be, not the mere fact that Gaddafi was removed from power.

Senators McCain and Graham, in the same breath, congratulated the rebels, the French, the Arabs, and the British. Then they said because we did not use our full airpower, President Obama had failed to remove Gaddafi sooner. If President Obama stayed out of this fight, Gaddafi would still be in power. But because President Obama made the decision to go forward with NATO, they could not congratulate him, only because he is a black man. Now if this president were a white man, he would have been a hero in their eyes.

No respect. No justice. No fairness. All we ask is for respect, justice, and fairness.

Today, if any citizen of this country makes a false statement under oath, they can be charged with perjury. If they make a false statement about someone, they can be sued. Most people, though, when someone tells them a lie and they find out about it, they never trust the person ever again.

Our politicians stand before us, telling lies and making false statements about a law or bill, knowing that they are lying; they are never held responsible for these lies. For instance, the lie told about President Obama's health care law: "there will be death panels."

Today, Republicans are using code words for racial issues: "welfare queens"; "taking our country back"; "going back to our forefathers' ways." Remember, most of our forefathers were slave owners. The new phrase from the right wing Republicans is that President Obama wants to divide our country with class warfare. Have you ever heard of segregation or Jim Crow laws? This country, from day one, has been divided. Can you also remember "White only" and "Colored only" signs? These code words send a frightening message to white people that President Obama is going to take this country from them and give it to black people.

In 2012, several white Republican presidential candidates accused President Obama of being the biggest "food stamp" president in history. "Food stamps" are code words for poor blacks. One candidate, Rick Santorum, told a white crowd, "We don't want to give black people your money; we want them to go to work and make their own money." These folks claim to represent all the citizens in the United States, but their rhetoric shows otherwise. Lastly, members of the Tea Party went to the capital of our nation for a rally, carrying guns; we ask ourselves why? Never before have people brought such shame to our country.

REPARATION: A MAKING OF AMENDS FOR ENSLAVING A NATION OF PEOPLE

When I hear black people ask for reparation from America for putting black people into slavery, I am offended. I will not accept any money for the crimes against my people. Now, I know there are millions of black people who would tell me to just speak for myself; this is just what I am doing: speaking for myself.

This money will never undo the millions of lives that were destroyed by this country. This would be blood money. If the millions of people who were kidnapped and forced into slavery could come back, then and only then could they be paid for their destroyed lives. They should be paid, not those of us who have never faced slavery.

If every black person in this country was given reparation for slavery, every criminal-minded person would know that their neighbors, coworkers, family members, and friends had money. This would only bring about the biggest crime spree in history; most of us would be murdered or robbed for our money. No one would go to work. This whole country would shut down. Afterward, most of us would have spent all of our money and we would be back where we started. This ultimately will be very sad.

Instead of reparation to black people, use this money to give all the people of our country the best education, and then make great jobs available to every man and woman, and pay them a fair wage. With a better educated population, crime goes down, so we as citizens could then make this great nation better than it is now; this is one idea to make our world a better place. With respect and fairness, by making the playing field level for everyone, we could start a movement. So why not start here?

PART IV. NOW AND THEN

CHAPTER 21

Reasons to Be Proud

IN THE BEGINNING GOD created man, a black man, and a black woman. This is why I am so proud to be a black man.

We were kidnapped from our humble existence, forced into slavery, sold as property, forced into free labor, and had our women and children raped. But we are still here, stronger than ever. The wealth of this country came from the labor of black people. So why am I so proud to be a black man?

There were millions of lives that paid the price for black people to be here in this country as free people. Black people are the paradigm. Why do you suppose I am so proud to be a black man?

Christians in the lions' den had nothing on black people during slavery, segregation, Jim Crow, and the Ku Klux Klan. At least the Christians' deaths were quick and did not last for hundreds of years. But after the terror of America's racial hatred, we are still here; thank you, God. This is one more reason why I am so proud to be a black man.

Before Europe came into existence, Egypt had gone through her twenty-fourth golden dynasty; the Moors were master builders who built the three pyramids of Giza and the Sphinx. Even today, with all our modern machines and technology, mankind still cannot duplicate them or explain how they were built.

Even after Egypt was old and tired her neighbor to her south, the Nubians (another black nation), ruled along with Egypt for another ten thousand years before there even was a Europe. These black Africans mapped the stars and even could tell the weight of our planet. Can you guess why I am so proud to be a black man?

Now let us take you inside these pyramids—secret tunnels and pathways that even today no one can explain how they carved them out with such precision. How could they see within these long chambers before electricity was invented? How did they get light enabling them to see down in the chambers and tunnels? How did they get air in the tunnels? They did not burn torches because there was no soot on the walls or ceilings. There are special chambers that the public is not even allowed to view. The Sphinx also has secret chambers. These black people achieved the unexplainable. Now, why am I proud to be a black man?

Afrique became Africa and the Nile Valley started social civilization. They set the standard of performance for the world but did not get credit for it.

Scientist, scholar, lecturer, and author Sheik Abidia Adebeys brought forth the black contributions from the mummies in Egypt.

Imhotep: Father of medicine in Egypt; 1800 years before the Greek father of medicine Akinakin. Why again am I so proud to be a black man?

The very first and only two universities devised by mankind were:

1. St. Noree—Timbuktu
2. Salamanca

They were created by black people and controlled later by Spain with Salamanca. You tell me, why am I so proud to be a black man?

From 1890 to 1908 they proceeded to pass legislation that disenfranchised most Negroes and many poor whites, trapping them without representation. They established white supremacist regimes of Jim Crow segregation in the South and one-party block voting behind southern Democrats.

The conservative whites denied African Americans their exercise of civil and political rights. The region's reliance on an agricultural economy continued to limit opportunities for most people. Negroes were exploited as sharecroppers and laborers.

After we were brought to America, not being able to speak English with no education, described as a beast in the fields, white America told the world that black people could not learn anything. But that is funny. So let us truly look at black people's history as black people wrote it themselves.

BLACK AUTHORS

Arna Bontemps. *God Sends Sundays* (1931), *Black Thunder* (1936).

Countee Cullen. *One Way to Heaven* (1932).

Jessie Redmon Fauset. *There Is Confusion* (1924), *Plum Bun* (1928), *The Chinaberry Tree* (1931), *Comedy, American-Style* (1933).

Rudolph Fisher. *The Walls of Jericho* (1928), *The Conjure-Man Dies* (1932).

Langston Hughes. *Not without Laughter* (1936).

Lora Neale Hurston. *Jonah's Guard Vine* (1934).

Nella Larsen. *Quicksand* (1928), *Passing* (1929).

Claude McKay. *Home to Harlem* (1927), *Banjo* (1929), *Ginger Town* (1931), *Banana Bottom* (1933).

George Schuyle. *Black No More* (1931), *Slaves Today* (1931).

Wallace Thurman. *The Blacker the Berry* (1929), *Infants of the Spring* (1932), *Interne* (1932).

Jean Toomer. *Cane* (1923).

Carl Van Vechten. *Nigger Heaven* (1926).

Walter White. *The Fire in the Flint* (1924), *Flight* (1926).

Why am I so proud to be a black man? You tell me.

LEADING INTELLECTUALS

1. W. E. B. Du Bois
2. Alain Locke
3. James Weldon Johnson
4. Charles Spurgeon Johnson
5. Walter White
6. Mary White Ovington
7. A. Philip Randolph
8. Chandler Owen
9. S. J. Joyce
10. William Stanley Braithwaite
11. Marcus Garvey
12. Joel Augustus Rogers
13. Marion Vera Cuthbert
14. Arthur Schomburg
15. Carl Van Vechten
16. Leslie Pinckney Hill
17. John Henrik Clarke

All are my people. Once again, why am I so proud to be a black man?

TUSKEGEE AIRMEN

The Tuskegee Airmen is the popular name of the group of African American pilots who fought in World War II. Formerly they were the 332nd fighter group and the 477th bombardment group of the US Army air Corps.

The Tuskegee Airmen were the first African American military aviators in the United States armed forces. During World War II African-Americans in many US states were still subject to racist Jim Crow laws. The American military was racially segregated, as was much of the federal government. The Tuskegee airmen were subject to racial discrimination, both within and outside the Army.

Despite these adversities, they trained and flew with distinction. Although the 477th bombardment group "worked up" on North

American B-25 Mitchell bombers, they never served in combat; the Tuskegee 332nd fighter group was the only operational unit first sent overseas as part of Operation Torch, then in action in Sicily and Italy before being deployed as bombers for white pilot escorts in Europe where they were particularly successful in their missions.

These white segregationist pilots wanted the Tuskegee pilots with their professional skills of flying as escorts for their protection. Tuskegee airmen were still black men, but yet these same racist, hateful white pilots did not want to go on their bombing missions unless the Tuskegee airmen flew alongside them. As these black fighter pilots flew on their missions protecting bomber crews word started spreading throughout about the skilled pilots and that all of the bomber crews made it back to home base safe. After over 50 missions the Tuskegee airmen never lost any bomber crews or planes. These black pilots went into harm's way doing their duty as Americans to save their country and fellow man; some had in their minds that the people they were protecting carried hatred in their hearts toward them, but these Tuskegee airmen conducted themselves in an honorable service, saving many airplanes and lives.

How many of the white crew's lives were saved by these black pilots and gave thanks to them?

The Tuskegee airmen initially were equipped with Curtis P-40 war hawks fighter bomber aircraft, briefly with Bell P-39 Airacobras (March 1944), later with Republic P-47 Thunderbolts (June-July 1944), and finally the fighter group acquired the aircraft with which they became most commonly associated, the North American P-51 Mustangs (July 1994). When the pilots of the 332nd Fighter Group painted the tails of their P-47s red; the nickname "Red Tails" was coined. Bomber crews called them "Red Tail Angels."

MORE REASONS AS TO WHY I AM SO PROUD.

Mrs. Henrietta Lacks – (He La) also Hela, or heta cell is a cell type and an immortal cell line used in scientific research. It is one of the oldest and most commonly used human cell lines. More reasons to be proud.

Because of this one Black woman modern medicine is where it is today.

Just Imagine life without any of these inventions

1. Air conditioning unit; just think about our lives without this unit, and what would life be like?
2. Auto cutoff switch; now if we could not turn it off our cars, Oh my Lord.
3. Baby buggy; oh my back, then how would we carry babies?
4. Bicycle frame; there goes Christmas; if there were no bicycle frames then what?
5. Blood plasma bag; let us count how many lives Mr. Drew has saved by his gift to the world; maybe even yours
6. Cellular phone; today everyone has a mobile phone we could not live without. Thanks you sir.
7. Chamber commode; just think how clean, healthy and convenient commodes are; what would all of us do if we had to have a bowel movement, there were no commodes available, it was midnight and 5 degrees below zero outside, and the only thing available was an outhouse.. Just thinking about this, just hurts my feeling. Here's a question. How many of those racist hateful, White people have a toilet in their homes or ever used a flushing toilet? Would they still have or used one if they knew a Black man invented it? Where would we all be if, Mr. T. Elkins were lynched, by hateful racist White people, just because he was a Black man?
8. Clothes dryer; I remember when most people couldn't afford a dryer, so we hung our clothing outside, on a clothes line. Today just imagine, if there were no clothes dryers and we had to go outside, to hang up all of our clothing, on the line; then when they are ready; you must go back outside and take them off the line, to bring them inside; can you guess what happened when it rained or it was very cold?
9. Elevator; how many times have you used an elevator? Can you imagine no elevators for a handicap person, to visit their doctor's office, or any multi-story building, large airport terminals, malls, etc.; trying to visit their granddaughter or grandson, requiring them to walk up fifty flights of stairs, while carrying groceries or other items.

10. Golf tee; what would Tiger Woods do; if there were no golf tee; I guess they would use a Coke can to hit these golf balls off.
11. Hairbrush; this hairbrush, strengthens our hair, shapes, beautifies our crowns.
12. Ironing board; just imagine if there were no ironing boards; I guess we would iron our clothes on the floor, or maybe on our tables.
13. Key chain; can you imagine, trying to keep up with all of your keys without this trusted tool?
14. Lawn mower; man if there were no lawnmowers, there goes my summer money; because when I was a kid, cutting people's lawns, was my way of making my summer money; and if there were no lawnmowers then people could not get to their front doors.
15. Locks; how safe we feel, when we are in our homes; and can lock our doors for security while we sleep.
16. Lubricating cup; every car and machinery that requires lubricating use this cup.
17. Refrigerator; this unit keeps our food fresh and cool; but if all of us did not have refrigerators, what kind of life would we have; my question is just imagine your home without any refrigeration? Why I Am So Proud to be a Black Man
18. Mailbox; every home and business has a mailbox. Yet no one tells us about these wonderful human, inventive beings; white America kept reminding people about how ignorant Black people are. Why I Am So Proud to be a Black Man.
19. Mop; without this mop, the world would have some very unclean floors.
20. Motor; every machine is run by a motor. Why I Am So Proud to be a Black Man.
21. Peanut butter; for all of you peanut butter lovers, you must give thanks to a Black man for this delicious treat. Why I Am So Proud to be a Black Man
22. Spark plug; every car and motor, without spark plugs in the whole world will come to a complete stop. It is just that simple; without spark plugs; you could not drive your car(s), or even

cut your lawn; oh my Lord. Why I Am So Proud to be a Black Man.

23. Stethoscope; every doctor and every nurse carries this medical miracle.

24. Traffic light; all around the world, there are traffic lights; just think how dangerous; it would be for us all if there were no traffic lights. Why I Am So Proud to be a Black Man.

25. Blood bank; this idea came from Dr. Charles Richard Drew 1904 through 1950; how many people lives have been saved by Dr. Drew, a Black Man. Dr. Drew's project was the model for the Red Cross system of blood banks, of which he became the first director. Why I Am So Proud to be a Black Man.

26. The potato chip was invented in 1853 by George Crum, a Black man. We all love a good chip. Why I Am So Proud to be a Black Man.

27. A laser based device to perform cataract surgery was by a Black woman. Why I Am So Proud to be a Black Man.

28. Accomplished the first successful open-heart surgery. Why I Am So Proud to be a Black Man.

If we take away any one of these great people, then we also must do without their great gifts to the world. Yet, today any one of these inventions would make you an instant billionaire as well as your family.

But the laws of this country at the time were wrong, cruel, and evil. How would you feel if someone took your life's work away from you and your family? Just imagine that every time you see a mailbox or a traffic light, the amount of money that was taken from you. There are so many of these cases that we as Black people in this country have had stolen from us; not just our freedom but our very soul.

This is a very painful emotion for any human being walking this Earth, carrying this heavy revelation about your own country.

Just imagine how repulsive this was. Recently in 2012 a church in Mississippi, a so-called house of God, refused to permit a couple, who were actual members of this church, to marry because they are black. The happy couple had made all of their arrangements and at the last minute the white minister of this predominately White church refused to do the ceremony. The members stated that permitting one black couple to marry may set a precedent meaning others may also want to get married there in their precious sacred church of God. What a shame.

Yet, these people have no shame by showing the world all their racist hatred for black people. Good old church folks, right?

There was no outcry from the people of this country when voter suppression laws were enacted from states that were under GOP control. Their lies regarding the changes were to stop voter fraud when in fact there were no cases of voter fraud. Sadly, the laws by these GOP runs states will deprive 5 million or more legal citizens of their rights to vote. So many have fought and given their lives for us all to have this precious right, which some mistakenly call a privilege. The 14th amendment protects all US citizens from deprivation of these rights, but because Congress is mostly dominated by the GOP, they just turn their heads away from doing their duty.

When someone calls them out, because their actions or words are racists, they in turn start telling you how many black friends they have, etc.; then turn right around and call you a racist because you call them out on it. When a white person (that 50% only) says something stupid, dumb, or racist, the rest of the racists come out and try to cover or explain to the public that we misunderstood what they were trying to say. So now, we as normal people are assumed to be so dumb they will attempt to explain what the person meant to say; they just used the wrong words and misspoke. Whew.

Now let's speak about Gabrielle "Gabby" Douglas. When she was about eight years old, she told her family that she wanted to do gymnastics. When she was fourteen years old, she began to train to become an Olympic gymnast.

There was a special gymnastic coach who trained students in Iowa; Gabby lived in the eastern part of the United States, far away from this particular coach. She knew that she needed to be trained by this special coach for the Olympic Games in 2012. So Gabby told her mother that she wanted to go to Iowa and train with this coach. Her mother explained that the family could not afford to move to Iowa. Gabby was persistent, and after giving it more thought, her mother said yes to her baby girl. Gabby's mother decided to let her fourteen-year-old daughter move to Iowa by herself.

Her mother found a family that would take Gabby in while she trained with the coach for the next two years. She absolutely knew this was the best person to train her for the 2012 Olympic Games. Take note that the family that allowed Gabby into their home was white.

The two families became one big family, for one cause, to see that their Gabby reached her goal. Two years later, at the Olympic Games, Gabby won the best all-around gymnast in the world. Also, for the very first time in history, a black American won a gold medal for being the world's best all-around gymnast.

These two families, Gabby's black family and her white family, together achieved something for the very first time. This sacrifice by both families showed what we as caring and compassionate people can do together as one nation, one people working together for our country.

We can achieve greatness together. This happened at a time when our nation needed this story of Gabby Douglas so badly. Two families, one white and one black, worked together, and guess what? No one looked at skin color. They simply exemplified the unity of love for this wonderful human being named Gabrielle Gabby Douglas; aka flying squirrel.

CHAPTER 22

Let Us Not Forget

MARTIN LUTHER KING JR.

Born: Michael King Jr., January 15, 1929, Atlanta, Georgia

Died: April 4, 1968 (age 39), in Memphis, Tennessee

Alma Mater: Morehouse College, Crozer Theological Seminary, Boston University

I still remember my first face-to-face meeting with Daddy King and Dr. Martin Luther King Jr., still watching his climb to lead the civil rights movement. I can still hear the words he spoke to me that day.

He led the 1955 Montgomery Bus Boycott, was a Nobel Peace Prize winner, and was posthumously awarded the Presidential Medal of Freedom.

In his "Letter from Birmingham Jail," Dr. King spoke of the injustice in America toward her own people. He spoke of many fathers and mothers looking into the eyes of their children with tears in their own eyes, trying to explain why black kids cannot go to the public library; why they can't go swimming like the white kids; and why white people treated black people so mean.

For his work to end racial segregation and discrimination through civil disobedience, he became the youngest person ever to receive the

Nobel Peace Prize. King was assassinated on April 4, 1968 in Memphis, Tennessee.

Montgomery Bus Boycott

In 1955, because of Jim Crow laws, fifteen-year-old Claudette Colvin, who was pregnant and unmarried, was required to give up her bus seat in Montgomery, Alabama, to a white man. She refused, and soon after, a similar case arose with Rosa Parks, who was arrested for the same offense. A bus boycott followed, lasting 385 days. It was so intense that King's house was bombed.

Soon afterward, the US District Court ruled in favor of the protesters, which ended racial segregation on all Montgomery public buses.

Southern Christian Leadership Conference

The SCLC was founded in 1957 by Dr. King and Ralph Abernathy. Its main purpose was to organize black churches to perform nonviolent protest for civil rights.

King's campaign implemented nonviolent techniques he learned by studying Indian leader Mohandas Gandhi. In the early 1960s, media coverage of the indignities inflicted on blacks by the southern Jim Crow laws led to a massive wave of sympathy from the general public, which in turn proved that the civil rights movement was the most important issue in the country.

The Civil Rights Act of 1964, which King worked tirelessly for, helped end segregation. It was followed by the Voting Rights Act of 1965.

Albany Movement

In November of 1961 in Albany, Georgia, a segregation group came together to confront every aspect of segregation. Using nonviolent tactics, King and the SCLC got involved and thousands participated.

King was subsequently arrested and ordered to pay a fine of $178. He chose to go jail, but the chief of police arranged for the fine to be paid so King could be released and leave the city.

St. Augustine, Florida and Selma, Alabama

In 1964, the SCLC and Dr. King were driving forces behind the protest in St. Augustine. Members of the movement were assaulted by white segregationists. Quite a few of the marchers were arrested and jailed.

By December 1964, the Student Nonviolent Coordinating Committee (SNCC) had been working on voter registration in Selma for several months; they were soon joined by the SCLC and Dr. King. A local judge barred any gathering of three or more people involved with SNCC or SCLC, and this injunction temporarily halted civil rights activity until King defied it by speaking at Brown Chapel.

March on Washington for Jobs and Freedom
Dr. King was one of the leaders of the Big Six civil rights organizations that were responsible for organizing the March on Washington on August 28, 1963. Other leaders and organizations comprising the Big Six were Roy Wilkins (NAACP); Whitney Young (National Urban League); A. Philip Randolph (Brotherhood of Sleeping Car Porters); John Lewis (SNCC); and James L. Farmer Jr. (Congress of Racial Equality).

President John F. Kennedy originally opposed the march because he felt it would create problems regarding the passage of civil rights legislation, but the marchers wanted to proceed and did so.

The famous "I Have a Dream" speech was given in front of the Lincoln Memorial during the 1963 March on Washington. The march originally was intended to dramatize the desperate condition of blacks in the South and question the government's failure to protect civil rights workers. But the marchers settled on a more subdued tone.

As a result, activists such as Malcolm X called it a Farce on Washington, and therefore the Nation of Islam forbade its members from attending.

Despite tensions, the march was a resounding success. More than a quarter million people of diverse ethnicities attended the event, sprawling from the steps of the Lincoln Memorial onto the National Mall and around the reflecting pool. It was the largest gathering of protesters in Washington's history. King's speech electrified the crowd. It is noted along with Abraham Lincoln's "Gettysburg Address" and Franklin D. Roosevelt's "Infamy" speech as one of the finest speeches in American history.

The March as well as King's speech help facilitate the passage of the Civil Rights Act of 1964.

From the Birmingham jail, Dr. King wrote explicitly about the oppressors of his time. His expressions of unjust treatment toward the Negro people haunted every fiber of his being.

Yet he was willing to go to jail for his convictions, telling all who would listen that an unjust law is no law at all. What are you willing to do to stand up for what you believe? You can research and discover for yourself what he stood tall for while incarcerated.

Bloody Sunday
Selma to Montgomery Marches
In March 1965, King, James Bevel, and the SCLC, in partial collaboration with SNCC, attempted to organize a march from Selma to Alabama's state capital in Montgomery. The first attempt on March 7 was aborted because of mob and police violence against the demonstrators. This day has since become known as Bloody Sunday. This was a major turning point in the effort to gain public support for the civil rights movement, the clearest demonstration up to that time of the dramatic potential of King's nonviolence strategy. King, however, was not present. King met with officials in the Johnson administration on March 5 in order to request an injunction against any prosecution of the demonstrators.

He did not attend the march due to church duties, but he later wrote, "If I had any idea that the state troopers would use the kind of brutality they did, I would have felt compelled to give up my church duties altogether to lead the line." Footage of police brutality against the protesters was broadcast extensively and aroused national public outrage.

King next attempted to organize a march on March 9. The SCLC petitioned for an injunction in federal court against the state of Alabama; this was denied, and the judge issued an order blocking the march until after the hearing. Nonetheless, King led a march on March 9 to the Edmund Pettus Bridge in Selma; he held a short prayer session before turning the marchers around and asking them to disperse so as not to violate the court order. The unexpected ending of the second march surprised and angered many within the local movement. The march finally went ahead on March 25. On the steps of the state capital,

King delivered a speech that has become known as "How Long? Not Long."

If you understand that oppression of any type can only survive for so long, you might ask how long will it take for mankind to realize we can accomplish so much more together than we can ever do apart.

Evolution is a natural step in the progress of any occurrence, so we must never accept the wrongs of others as the norm. When the student is ready, the teacher will always appear.

Legacy

Rev. Martin Luther King Jr.'s legacy was to secure progress on civil rights in the United States, which has enabled more Americans to reach their potential. He is frequently referenced as a human rights icon today. His name and legacy have often been invoked since his death as people have debated his likely position on various modern political issues.

On the international scene, King's legacy included influences on the black consciousness movement and the civil rights movement in South Africa. King's work was cited as an inspiration for South African leader Albert Lutuli, another black Nobel Peace Prize winner, who fought for racial justice in his country.

Coretta Scott King followed her husband's footsteps and was active in matters of social justice and civil rights until her death in 2006. The same year that King was assassinated, she established the King Center in Atlanta, dedicated to preserving his legacy and the work of championing nonviolent conflict resolution and tolerance worldwide. Their son, Dexter King, currently serves as the center's chairman. Yolanda King, who died in 2007, was a motivational speaker, author, and founder of Higher Ground Productions, an organization specializing in diversity training.

Even within the King family, there are opposing views of the slain civil rights leader's religious and political views about homosexuality. Coretta said publicly that she believed he would have been opposed to gay marriage. The King Center includes facts regarding discrimination, and homophobia is on its list of the "Triple Evils" that should be opposed.

In 1980, the Department of the Interior designated King's boyhood home in Atlanta and several nearby buildings as the Martin Luther King Jr. National Historic Site. In 1996, Congress authorized the Alpha Phi

Alpha fraternity to establish a foundation to raise funds for the design of a Martin Luther King National Memorial on the National Mall in Washington DC. King was the first African American honored with a memorial on the mall and the first non-president to be commemorated in such a way. The King Memorial is administered by the National Park Service.

King's life and assassination inspired many artistic works. In 1976, a Broadway production entitled *I Have a Dream* starred Billy Dee Williams as King. In the spring of 2006, a stage play about King was produced in Beijing, China, with King portrayed by Chinese actor Cao Li. The play was written by a Stanford University professor, Clayborne Carson.

Before his death, King spoke about what people should remember him for if they were around for his funeral. He said rather than his awards and where he went to school, people should talk about how he fought peacefully for justice.

"I would like somebody to mention that day that Martin Luther King Jr. tried to give his life serving others," he said. "I would like for somebody to say that day that Martin Luther King Jr. tried to love somebody. I want you to say that day that I tried to be right on the war question. I want you to be able to say that day that I did try to feed the hungry. I want you to be able to say that day that I did try in my life to clothe those who were naked. I want you to say on that day that I tried in my life to visit those who were in prison. And I want you to say that I tried to love and serve humanity. Yes, if you want to say that I was a drum major, say that I was a drum major for justice. Say that I was a drum major for peace. I was a drum major for righteousness. And all of the shallow things will not matter."

Martin Luther King Jr. Day
On November 2, 1983, President Reagan signed a bill creating a federal holiday to honor King. Martin Luther King Jr. Day was observed for the first time on January 20, 1986. Following President George H. W. Bush's 1992 proclamation, the holiday is observed on the third Monday of January each year, near the time of King's birthday. On January 17, 2000, for the first time Martin Luther King Jr. Day was officially observed in all fifty US states; Arizona (1992), New Hampshire (1999),

and Utah (2000) were the last three states to recognize the holiday. Awards and recognition statues of King are in Birmingham's Kelly Ingram Park.

King was awarded at least fifty honorary degrees from colleges and universities in the United States and elsewhere. In 1965, King was awarded the American Liberties Medallion by Jewish Americans for his exceptional advancement of the principles of liberty. In his acceptance remarks, King said, "Freedom is one thing. You have it all or you are not free."

King was second in Gallup's list of widely admired people in the twentieth century. In 1963, he was named *Time* magazine's man of the year, and in 2000, he was voted sixth in the Person of the Century poll by the same magazine. King was selected third greatest American in a contest conducted by the Discovery Channel and AOL. More than 730 cities in the United States have streets named after King. King County, Washington, rededicated its name in his honor in 1986 and changed its logo to an image of his face in 2007. King is remembered as a martyr by the Episcopal Church in the United States of America (feast day, April 4) and the Evangelical Lutheran Church in America (feast day, January 15).

In 2002, scholar Molefi Kete Asante named King on his list of *100 Greatest African Americans*.

RALPH ABERNATHY

Born: March 11, 1926

Died: April 17, 1990

Ralph David Abernathy Sr. was a leader of the American civil rights movement, a minister, and a close associate of Dr. Martin Luther King Jr. in the Southern Christian Leadership Conference. Following King's assassination, Dr. Abernathy took up the leadership of the SCLC Poor People's Campaign and led the March on Washington that had been planned for May 1968.

As an officer of the Montgomery NAACP, he organized the first mass meeting of the Montgomery Bus Boycott to protest Rosa Parks' arrest. In the beginning of the civil rights movement, Dr. Abernathy led the largest black church, First Baptist Church.

At the end of the boycott, on January 10, 1957, Dr. Abernathy's church and his home were severely bombed; his wife, Juanita, and infant daughter, Juandalyan, were unharmed.

In his last speech, "I've Been to the Mountaintop," Dr. Martin Luther King Jr. said that Ralph Abernathy was the best friend he had in the world. They first met in Atlanta while still in school and formed a lifelong friendship and partnership, which ended on April 4, 1968, when King was shot in Memphis. In his 1989 memoir, *And the Walls Came Tumbling Down*, Abernathy recounts in some detail what he calls King's womanizing. King was alone late into the night with several different women at the Lorraine Motel in Memphis on the very night before his assassination, according to Abernathy.

Civil Rights Work

On December 2, 1955, in response to the arrest of Rosa Parks, Abernathy and King organized the Montgomery Bus Boycott and cofounded the American civil rights movement. The Montgomery Improvement Association led the successful transit boycott, challenging Jim Crow segregation laws and ending Alabama's bus segregation.

While actively involved in the beginning of the civil rights movement, he completed his master's degree in sociology at Atlanta University. His master's thesis, "The Natural History of a Social Movement: The Montgomery Improvement Association," was included in David Garrow's book, *The Walking City: The Montgomery Bus Boycott, 1955–1956*.

Dr. Abernathy served as SCLC's financial secretary, treasurer, and vice president while Dr. King was its president, and he assumed the presidency upon Dr. King's death.

The Abernathy/King partnership spearheaded successful nonviolent movements in Montgomery, Albany, Birmingham, Mississippi, Washington, Selma, St. Augustine, Chicago, and Memphis. Their work helped to secure the passage of the landmark Civil Rights Act of 1964 and the Voting Rights Act of 1965, and the abolition of Jim Crow segregation laws in the southern United States.

In May 1968, Abernathy led the Poor People's Campaign in

Washington DC. The nation's poor blacks, Latinos, whites, and Native Americans came together from the Mississippi Delta, the Blue Ridge Mountains, the Indian reservations of the Northwest, the farmlands of the Southwest, and the inner cities of the North under the leadership of Dr. Abernathy to form Resurrection City on the mall of the Washington Memorial. Hoping to bring attention to the plight of the nation's impoverished they constructed the makeshift city in the nation's capital, precipitating a showdown with the police. On June 19, Abernathy spoke at the Lincoln Memorial in front of tens of thousands of black and white citizens.

The Poor People's Campaign reflected Abernathy's deep conviction that the "key to salvation and redemption of this nation lay in its moral and humane response to the needs of this most oppressed and poverty-stricken citizens." His aim in the spring of 1968 was to raise the nation's consciousness on hunger and poverty, which he achieved. The Poor People's Campaign led to systematic changes in US federal policies and legislation creating a national food stamp program, a free meal program for low income children, assistance programs for the elderly, work programs, and day care and health care programs for low income people across America. On June 24, 1968, the Washington DC police forced the protestors to disband and demolished Resurrection City.

Abernathy was jailed for nearly three weeks for refusing to comply with orders to evacuate. During his lifetime, Abernathy was honored with more than 300 awards and citations, including five honorary doctorate degrees (he received honorary degrees from Long Island University in New York, Morehouse College in Atlanta, Kalamazoo College in Michigan, and his alma mater, Alabama State University in Montgomery). He served as a representative of the National Council for the Aged, the World Commission on Hunger, the NAACP, the Progressive National Baptist Convention, the American Sociological Society, Kappa Alpha Psi fraternity, the Atlanta Baptist Ministers Union, and more than forty other organizations. An advocate of the Constitution's First Amendment for religious freedom, Dr. Abernathy served as vice president along with Dr. Robert Grant and cofounded the American Freedom Coalition in 1980.

On April 17, 1990, Abernathy died at Emory Crawford Long Memorial Hospital from two blood clots that traveled to his heart and lungs. Abernathy Road in southwest Atlanta, a portion of Interstate 20, and Ralph David Abernathy Boulevard of Atlanta were named in his honor.

His son, Ralph David Abernathy III, is a social activist who heads a community foundation that funds education and health and wellness programs in African American communities, as well as efforts toward prison reform.

MAYNARD HOLBROOK JACKSON JR.

Born: March 23, 1938

Died: June 23, 2003

Maynard Holbrook Jackson Jr. was the first African American mayor of Atlanta. He served two consecutive terms from 1974 until 1982 and a third term from 1990 to 1994. He was elected mayor in the same week that Coleman Young became the first African American mayor of Detroit.

Jackson's grandfather was the civil rights leader John Wesley Dobbs. His mother, Irene Dobbs Jackson, was a professor of French at Spelman College in Atlanta. In 1956, Jackson graduated from Morehouse College when he was only eighteen years old; he sang in the Morehouse College Glee Club. After attending Boston University Law School for a short time, he held several jobs, including selling encyclopedias, before he enrolled in North Carolina Central University Law School, from which he graduated in 1964. He was a member of Alpha Phi Alpha fraternity.

Mayor of Atlanta
During Jackson's first term as mayor, progress was made in improving race relations, and Atlanta became known as "the city too busy to hate." As mayor, he led several huge public works projects in the region. He helped arrange for the rebuilding of Hartsfield Atlanta International Airport; shortly after his death, the airport was renamed the Hartsville-Jackson Atlanta International Airport in his honor.

Jackson was mayor when Atlanta was selected as the host city for the 1996 Summer Olympic Games. He attended the 1992 closing ceremonies in Barcelona, Spain, and accepted the Olympic flag.

Emotions were high when Jackson was elected mayor of Atlanta; for the first time in our lives, we had a mayor that looked like us, black people. Our city changed overnight, just like when Barack Obama was elected president. Our city became a city of lights. Mayor Jackson put Atlanta on the map.

John Lewis

Born: February 21, 1940-

In 1987, John Lewis was elected to represent Georgia's fifth congressional district. He was a leader in the American civil rights movement and chairman of the Student Nonviolent Coordinating Committee, playing a key role in the struggle to end segregation.

Lewis was an influential SNCC leader and is recognized as one of the important leaders of the civil rights movements as a whole. He was a hard-working young man who overcame poverty and political disenfranchisement to get a good education.

He graduated from the American Baptist Theological Seminary in Nashville and received a bachelor's degree in religion and philosophy from this university. As a student, Lewis was very dedicated to the civil rights movement. He organized a sit-in at segregated lunch counters in Nashville and took part in many other civil rights activities.

In 1961, Lewis joined SNCC in the Freedom Rides, which challenged segregation at interstate bus terminals in the South. Lewis and others received death threats and were severely beaten by angry mobs. In 1963, when Chuck McDew stepped down as SNCC chairman, Lewis was quickly elected to take over. His experience at that point was already widely respected, and he had been arrested twenty-four times as a result of his activism. He held the post of chairman until 1966.

In 1963, Lewis helped plan the March on Washington. At the age of twenty-three, he was a keynote speaker at the historic event. In 1964, Lewis coordinated SNCC's efforts for "Mississippi Freedom Summer," a campaign to register black voters across the South. Lewis became nationally known during his prominent role in the Selma to Montgomery marches.

In 1965, he led marchers across the Pettus Bridge in Selma, Alabama. The state troopers attacked the marchers in a violent incident that later became known as "Bloody Sunday." He endured beatings by angry mobs and suffered a fractured skull at the hands of Alabama state police.

Before he could be taken to the hospital, Lewis appeared before the television cameras, calling on President Johnson to intervene. Lewis bears scars on his head that are still visible today.

"We were determined not to let any act of violence keep us from our goal. We knew our lives could be threatened, but we had made up our minds not to turn back," Lewis said recently in regard to his perseverance following the act of violence.

Lewis said, "I saw racial discrimination as a young child. I saw those signs that said, 'White men,' 'Colored men,' 'White women,' 'Colored women.' I remember as a young child with some of my brothers and sisters and first cousins going down to the public library and trying to get library cards, trying to check some books out, and we were told by the librarian that the library was for whites only and not for coloreds."

In 1981, Lewis was elected as an Atlanta City Council member. In 1986, he was elected to Congress, where he is currently serving his thirteenth term.

In an interview with CNN during the fortieth anniversary of the Freedom Rides, Lewis recounted the sheer amount of violence he and the other original Freedom Riders endured. In Anniston, Alabama, their bus was fire-bombed by Ku Klux Klan members. In Birmingham, the riders were mercilessly beaten, and in Montgomery, an angry mob met the bus, where Lewis was hit in the head with a wooden crate. "It was very violent. I thought I was going to die. I was left behind at the Greyhound bus station in Montgomery unconscious," Lewis said, remembering the incident. The original intent of the Freedom Riders was to test the new laws that banned segregation in public transportation. It also exposed the passivity of the government regarding violence against citizens of the country who were simply acting in accordance to the law.

JOSEPH LOWERY

Born: October 6, 1921-

Huntsville, Alabama

Organizations: Southern Christian Leadership Conference; Alabama Civic Affairs Association; Black Leadership Forum; Lowery Institute

Spouse: Evelyn G. Lowery

Awards: Presidential Medal of Freedom (2009)

Joseph Echols Lowery is a minister in the United Methodists Church and a leader in the American civil rights movement. He later became the third president of the Southern Christian Leadership Conference after Dr. Martin Luther King Jr. and his immediate successor, Rev. Ralph Abernathy, and participated in most of the major activities of the African American civil rights movement of the 1960s.

From 1952 until 1961, Lowery was pastor of the Warren Street United Methodist Church in Mobile, Alabama. His career in the civil rights movement began in the 1950s in Mobile. After Rosa Parks' arrest in 1955, Lowery helped lead the Montgomery Bus Boycott. He headed the Alabama Civil Affairs Association, an organization devoted to the desegregation of buses and public places. In 1957, along with King, Lowery founded the Southern Christian Leadership Conference and subsequently led the organization as its president from 1977 to 1997.

In 1959, Lowery's property was seized by the state of Alabama as part of the settlement of a libel suit. The Supreme Court later reversed this decision. At the request of Dr. King, Lowery led the march from Selma to Montgomery in 1965. Lowery is a cofounder and former president of the Black Leadership Forum, a consortium of black advocacy groups.

This forum protested the apartheid system of white-minority rule in South Africa until it finally ended. Lowery was arrested outside the South African Embassy in Washington DC during the Free South Africa movement. From 1986 through 1992, Lowery served as the pastor of Cascade United Methodist Church in Atlanta, adding over one thousand members.

Lowery is now retired from the ministry, but he remains active in the civil rights movement and in Christian activities.

To honor Rev. Lowery, Atlanta renamed Ashby Street for him. Joseph E. Lowery Boulevard runs past Atlanta's historically black colleges and universities: Clark Atlanta University, Spelman College, Morehouse College, and Morris Brown College. This street intersects both Martin Luther King Jr. Drive and the Ralph David Abernathy Expressway.

Rev. Lowery has advocated for LGBT civil rights, including civil unions and same-sex marriage.

ANDREW YOUNG

Born: March 12, 1932-

Andrew Young is an American politician, diplomat, activist, and pastor from Georgia. He served as mayor of Atlanta, was a congressman from the Fifth District, and was US ambassador to the United Nations. He served as president of the National Council of Churches USA, was a member of the Southern Christian Leadership Conference during the 1960s civil rights movement, and was a supporter and friend of Dr. Martin Luther King Jr.

Early Life
Young was born in New Orleans to Daisy Fuller Young, a schoolteacher, and Andrew Jackson Young Sr., a dentist. Young's father hired a professional boxer to teach Andrew and his brother how to fight so they could defend themselves. After that, Young decided that violence was not the path he would choose to follow.

Education
After beginning his higher education at Dillard University, Young transferred to Howard University in Washington DC in 1947 and received his Bachelor of Science degree there in 1951. He originally had planned to follow his father's career of dentistry but then felt a religious calling.

He entered the Turner-Boatright Christian Ministries School and in 1955 earned a bachelor of divinity degree from Hartford Seminary in Hartford, Connecticut.

Young was appointed to serve as pastor of a church in Marion County, Alabama. In Marion, he met Jean Childs, who later became his wife. Also while in Marion, Young began to study the writing of Mohandas Gandhi. Young became interested in Gandhi's concept of nonviolent resistance as a tactic for social change. He encouraged African Americans to register to vote in Alabama, often facing death threats while doing so.

However, as the civil rights movement gained momentum, Young decided that his place was back in the South. In 1960, he joined the Southern Christian Leadership Conference. In 1961, he and Jean moved to Atlanta and continued registering black voters. Young was jailed for his participation in civil rights demonstrations in Selma, Alabama, and in St. Augustine, Florida. He played a key role in the events in Birmingham, serving as a mediator between the white and black communities. In 1964, Young was named executive director of the SCLC, becoming one of Dr. Martin Luther King Jr.'s principal lieutenants.

As a colleague and friend to King, he was a strategist and negotiator during the civil rights campaigns in Birmingham (1963), St. Augustine (1964), Selma (1965), and Atlanta (1966). He was with King in Memphis when he was assassinated in 1968.

Political Career

In 1970, Andrew Young ran for Congress in Georgia but was unsuccessful. After his defeat, Rev. Fred C. Bennette Jr. introduced him to Murray M. Silver, an attorney from Atlanta who promoted concerts featuring top entertainers, including Harry Belafonte and Bill Withers. Silver served as Young's campaign finance chairman, and he ran again in 1972 and won. He later was reelected in 1974 and 1976.

During his four-plus years in Congress, he was a member of the Congressional Black Caucus and was involved in several debates regarding foreign relations.

ADAM CLAYTON POWELL JR.

Born: November 29, 1908

Died: April 4, 1972 (age 63)

Adam Clayton Powell Jr. was an American politician and pastor who represented Harlem in the US House of Representatives (1945–1971). He was the first African American elected to Congress from New York and became a powerful national politician. In 1961, after sixteen years in the House, he became chairman of the Education and Labor Committee.

As chairman, he supported the passage of important legislation under Presidents John F. Kennedy and Lyndon B. Johnson. Following allegations of corruption, he was excluded from his seat by Democrats but was reelected; he regained the seat in a 1969 United States Supreme Court ruling.

Powell grew up in a wealthy household in New York City. He attended Townsend Harris High School. As an undergraduate, he studied at the City College of New York and Colgate University. He was one of five African American students at Colgate (and the only nonathlete), and for a time he passed as white in dating before deciding to identify as black. Encouraged by his father to follow him as a minister, Powell got more serious about his studies at Colgate. He earned a master's in religious education from Columbia University in 1931. He was a member of Alpha Phi Alpha.

Career
After ordination, Powell began assisting his father with charitable services at Abyssinian Baptist Church, and as a preacher, he greatly enlarged the volume of meals and clothing provided to the needy. He also began to learn more about the lives of the working class and poor in Harlem. During the Great Depression in the 1930s, Powell, a handsome and charismatic figure, became a prominent civil rights leader. He developed a formidable public following in Harlem through his crusades for jobs and affordable housing. As chairman of the Coordinating Committee for Employment, he used numerous methods of community organizing to bring political pressure on major businesses to hire black employees

at professional levels. He organized mass meetings, rent strikes, and public campaigns to force companies, utilities, and Harlem Hospital to hire skilled black workers.

During the 1939 World's Fair, Powell organized a picket line at the fair's offices in the Empire State Building; as a result, the number of black employees was increased from about 200 to 732. In 1941, he led a bus boycott in Harlem; the Transit Authority hired 200 black workers. Powell also led a fight to have drugstores operating in Harlem hire black pharmacists, and he encouraged residents to shop where blacks worked. In 1938, he succeeded his father as pastor of the Abyssinian Baptist Church.

Political Career

In 1941, Powell was elected to the New York City Council as the city's first black representative. He received 65,736 votes, the third best total among the candidates.

"Mass action is the most powerful force on earth," Powell once said. "As long as it is within the law, it's not wrong; if the law is wrong, change the law."

In 1944, Powell ran for Congress on a platform rights for African Americans: support for fair employment practices, and a ban on poll taxes and lynching. He was elected to represent the congressional district that included Harlem. He was the first black congressman from New York State and the first in the post-Reconstruction era from any northern state other than Illinois. Powell challenged the informal ban on black representatives using Capitol facilities reserved for white members. He often took black constituents to dine with him in the whites-only House restaurant.

He clashed with many of the segregationists in his party. Since the late nineteenth century, southern Democrats commanded a one-party system in most of the South, as they had effectively disenfranchised most blacks from voting. White congressmen controlled all the seats allocated for the southern states and commanded many important committee chairs in the House and Senate. Powell worked closely with Clarence Mitchell, the NAACP representative in Washington, to try to gain justice and increase federal programs. Historian Charles Hamilton described the NAACP as "the quarterback that threw the ball to Powell, who, to his credit, was more than happy to catch and run with it." He developed a strategy known as the Powell amendments. On bill after bill that proposed federal expenditures, Powell would offer customary amendments denying federal funds to any jurisdiction that maintained segregation. Liberals were embarrassed, and southern politicians angered.

This principle became integrated into the Civil Rights Act of 1964. In 1961, after fifteen years in Congress, Powell became chairman of the powerful Education and Labor Committee. In this position he presided over federal social programs for minimum wage and Medicaid (established later under Johnson); he expanded the minimum wage to include retail workers and worked for equal pay for women; he supported education and training for the deaf, nursing education, and vocational training; he led legislation for standards for wages and work hours, as well as for aid for elementary and secondary education and school libraries. Powell was instrumental in passing legislation that made lynching a federal crime, as well as bills that desegregated public schools.

He challenged the southern practice of charging blacks a poll tax to vote, but electoral practices were not changed substantially in most of the South until after passage of the Voting Rights Act of 1965, which provided federal oversight of voter registration and elections.

Death

In 1972, Powell became gravely ill and was flown to a Miami hospital from his home in Bimini. He died there from acute prostatitis, according to newspaper accounts. After his funeral at the Abyssinian Baptist Church in Harlem, his son Adam III poured his ashes from a plane over the waters of his beloved Bimini.

FRED SHUTTLESWORTH

Born: Freddie Lee Robinson, 1922, Mount Meigs, Alabama

Died: October 5, 2011 (age 89)

Organization: Alabama Christian Movement for Human Rights

Rev. Fred Shuttlesworth was a US civil rights activist who led the fight against segregation and other forms of racism as a minister in

Birmingham, Alabama. He was a cofounder of the Southern Christian Leadership Conference, was instrumental in the 1963 Birmingham campaign, and continued to work against racism and for the homeless in Cincinnati, Ohio, where he took up a pastorate in 1961. He returned to Birmingham after his retirement in 2007.

The Birmingham Airport is named after him. He was intensely involved in the Birmingham struggle after moving to Cincinnati and frequently returned to help lead actions.

Shuttlesworth personally feared for his life, even though he was aware of the risk he ran. Other committed activists were scared off or mystified by his willingness to accept the risk of death. Shuttlesworth himself vowed to kill segregation or be killed by it.

Southern Christian Leadership Conference
In 1957, Shuttlesworth along with Dr. Martin Luther King Jr., Rev. Ralph Abernathy (from Montgomery), Rev. Joseph Lowery (from Mobile, Alabama), Rev. T. J. Jemison (from Baton Rouge, Louisiana), Rev. C. K. Steele (from Tallahassee, Florida), Rev. A. L. Davis (from New Orleans, Louisiana), Bayard Rustin, and Ella Baker founded the Southern Leadership Conference on Transportation and Nonviolent Integration, later renamed the Southern Christian Leadership Conference. The SCLC adopted a motto to underscore its commitment to nonviolence: "Not one hair of one head of one person should be harmed."

Shuttlesworth embraced that philosophy, even though his own personality was combative, headstrong, and sometimes blunt, to the point that he frequently antagonized his colleagues in the movement. He was not shy in asking King to take a more active role in leading the fight against segregation and warning that history would not look kindly on those who gave "flowery speeches" but did not act on them. He alienated some members of his congregation by devoting as much time as he did to the civil rights movement, at the expense of weddings, funerals, and ordinary church functions. As a result, in 1961 Shuttlesworth moved to Cincinnati to take up the pastorage of the Revelation Baptist Church.

Project C
In 1963, Shuttlesworth invited SCLC and Dr. King to come to Birmingham to lead a desegregation campaign; Shuttlesworth called

it Project C (the C stood for confrontation). While Shuttlesworth was willing to negotiate with political and business leaders for peaceful abandonment of segregation, he believed with good reason that they would not take any steps unless they were forced to. He suspected their promises could not be trusted on until they acted on them.

One of the demonstrations he led resulted in Shuttlesworth being convicted of parading without a permit. On appeals, the case reached the US Supreme Court. In its 1969 decision of *Shuttlesworth versus Birmingham*, the Supreme Court reversed Shuttleworth's conviction. They determined circumstances indicated that the parade permit was not denied to control traffic, as the state contended. After the Voting Rights Act, Shuttlesworth organized the Greater New Light Baptist Church in Cincinnati.

In 1978, Shuttlesworth was portrayed by Roger Robinson in the television miniseries *King*. Shuttlesworth founded the Shuttlesworth Housing Foundation in 1988 to assist families who might otherwise be unable to buy their own homes.

In 1998, Shuttlesworth became a supporter of the Birmingham Lineage, a grassroots community committed to combating racism and prejudice. It has since been used for programs in all fifty states and more than twenty countries.

On January 8, 2001, he was presented with the Presidential Citizen's Medal by President Bill Clinton. Named president of the Southern Christian Leadership Conference in August 2004, he resigned later in the year, complaining that deceit, mistrust, and a lack of spiritual discipline and truth had eaten at the core of this once hallowed organization.

ALTHEA GIBSON

Born: August 25, 1927, Clarendon County, South Carolina

Died: September 28, 2003 (age 76) in East Orange, New Jersey

Althea Gibson was a world-class sportswoman who became the first African American woman on the world tennis tour; she won a Grand Slam title in 1956. She is sometimes referred to as the Jackie Robinson of tennis for breaking the color barrier.

According to Lance Tingay of the *Daily Telegraph,* Gibson was ranked in the top ten from 1956 through 1958; she was number one in the world in 1957 and 1958. In 1957, Althea became the first African American woman to win Wimbledon. She won again in 1958, and after she retired, Gibson wrote her autobiography. In 1959, she recorded an album, *Althea Gibson Sings,* and appeared in the motion picture *The Horse Soldiers.* In 1964, she became the first African American woman to play in the Ladies Professional Golf Association. However, she only played for a few years.

In 1971, Gibson was inducted into the International Tennis Hall of Fame, and in 1975, she was appointed New Jersey State Commissioner of Athletics. In 1977, she challenged incumbent Essex County State Senator Frank J. Dodd in the Democratic primary for his seat. She came in second behind Dodd, but ahead of Assemblyman Eldridge Hawkins. After ten years as commissioner, she went on to work in public service positions, including serving on the Governor's Council on Physical Fitness.

In later years, Gibson called her former doubles partner, Angela Buxton, and told her she was considering suicide, as she was living on welfare and unable to pay for rent or medication.

Buxton wrote a letter to a tennis magazine, explaining Gibson's plight and seeking donations. She told Gibson nothing about the letter, but magazine received nearly $1 million from around the world.

Gibson was married twice. Her first marriage to William Darben took place in 1965; the couple was divorced in 1976. She also married Sydney Liewellyn in 1983 and was divorced from him in 1988. In 2003, Gibson died in East Orange, New Jersey, due to circulatory failure.

On the opening night of the 2007 US Open, the fiftieth anniversary of Gibson's victory in 1957, she was inducted into the US Open Court of Champions. She was a 1994 inductee of the Sports Hall of Fame of the New Jersey Hall of Fame. In September 2009, the city of Wilmington, North Carolina, named its new community tennis complex the Althea Gibson Tennis Center.

ARTHUR ASHE

Born: July 10, 1943, Richmond, Virginia

Died: February 6, 1993 (age 49) in New York City

Arthur Robert Ashe Jr. was a professional tennis player, born and raised in Richmond, Virginia. During his career he won three Grand Slam titles, putting him among the best ever from the United States. Ashe was the first black player ever selected to the US Davis Cup team and the only black man to ever win the singles title Wimbledon, the US Open, and the Australian Open. He is also remembered for his efforts to further social causes.

After retiring from professional tennis, Ashe wrote for *Time* magazine, commentated for ABC Sports, found the National Junior Tennis League, and served as captain of the US Davis Cup team. In 1983, Ashe underwent heart surgery for the second time. He was elected to the International Tennis Hall of Fame in 1985. He also founded the Arthur Ashe Foundation for the defeat of AIDS.

Here are some facts about Ashe's successes: career titles: 33; highest ranking: number one in 1969; Grand Slam results: won the Australian Open in 1970; reached quarterfinals of the French Open in 1970–1971; won Wimbledon in 1975; won the US Open in 1968. He won fourteen titles and earned $1,584,909, according to the ATP.

HARRIET TUBMAN

Born: March 1822

Died: March 19, 1913

Tubman was an African American abolitionist, humanitarian, and unionist during the American Civil War. After escaping from slavery, into which she was born, she made thirteen missions to rescue more than seventy slaves, using the network of antislavery activists and safe houses known as the Underground Railroad. She later helped John Brown recruit men for his raid on Harper's Ferry, and in the postwar era, she joined the struggle for women's suffrage.

In 1849, Tubman escaped to Philadelphia and then immediately returned to Maryland to rescue her family. Slowly, one group at a time, she brought relatives out of the state and eventually guided dozens of other slaves to freedom. Traveling by night, Tubman (or Moses, as she was called) never lost a passenger. Large rewards were offered for the return of many of the fugitive slaves, but no one knew that Tubman was the one helping them. When the southern-dominated Congress passed the Fugitive State Law of 1850, requiring law officials in free states to aid efforts to recapture slaves, she helped guide fugitives further north into Canada, where slavery was prohibited.

Rosa Louise McCauley Parks

Born: February 4, 1913

Died: October 24, 2005

Parks was an African American civil rights activist who was called "the First Lady of civil rights" and the mother of the freedom movement.

On December 1, 1955, in Montgomery, Alabama, Parks refused to obey bus driver James Blake's order that she give up her seat to make room for a white passenger. Parks' action was not the first of its kind to impact the civil rights issue, but her civil disobedience sparked the Montgomery Bus Boycott. Stand up against injustice.

Parks' act of defiance became an important symbol of the modern civil rights movement, and she became an international icon of resistance to racial segregation. She organized and collaborated with civil rights leaders, including Martin Luther King Jr., helping to launch him to national prominence in the civil rights movement.

Malcolm X

Born: Malcolm Little, May 19, 1925, Omaha, Nebraska

Died: February 21, 1965

Malcolm X was also known as El-Hajj El Shabazz; he was an African American Muslim minister, public speaker, and human rights activist.

To his admirers, he was a courageous advocate for the rights of African Americans, a man who indicted white America in the harshest terms for its crimes against black Americans. His detractors accused him of preaching racism, black supremacy, anti-Semitism, and violence. He has been called one of the greatest and most influential African Americans in history, and in 1998, *Time* magazine named *The Autobiography of Malcolm X* one of the ten most influential nonfiction books of the twentieth century.

DOROTHY HEIGHT

Born: March 24, 1912, Richmond, Virginia

Died: April 20, 2010 (age 98) in Washington, DC

Dorothy Irene Height was an American educator and social activist. She was the president of the National Council of Negro Women for forty years and was awarded the Presidential Medal of Freedom in 1994 and the Congressional Gold Medal in 2004.

Early Life
At a very early age, Height moved with her family to Rankin, Pennsylvania, a steel town in the suburbs of Pittsburgh. Height was admitted to Barnard College in 1929, but upon arrival, she was denied entrance because the school had an unwritten policy of limiting only two black students per year. She pursued studies instead at New York University, earning a degree in 1932, and a master's degree in educational psychology the following year.

Career
Height started working as a caseworker with the New York City Welfare Department, and at the age of twenty-five, she began a career as a civil rights activist when she joined the National Council of Negro Women. She fought for equal rights for African Americans and all women, and in 1944, she joined the national staff of the YWCA. She also served as national president of Delta Sigma Theta sorority from 1946 to 1957. She remained active with the sorority throughout leadership training programs and interracial and ecumenical education programs.

In 1957, Height was named president of the National Council of Negro Women, a position she held until 1997. During the height of the civil rights movement of the 1960s, Height organized "Wednesdays in Mississippi," which brought together black and white women from the North and South to create a dialogue of understanding.

American leaders regularly took her counsel, including First Lady Eleanor Roosevelt; Height encouraged President Dwight D. Eisenhower to desegregate schools and President Lyndon B. Johnson to appoint African American women to positions in government. In the mid-1960s, Height wrote a column entitled "A Woman's Word" for the weekly African American newspaper, the *New York Amsterdam News*.

Height worked as a consultant on African affairs for the secretary of state and served on the President's Committee on the Employment of the Handicapped and the President's Committee on the Status of Women. In 1974, Height was named to the National Council for the Protection of Human Subjects of Biomedical and Behavioral Research, which published a response to the infamous "Tuskegee Syphilis Study." The Belmont Report remains an ethical touchstone for researchers to this day.

The Dorothy J. Height Building, headquarters of the National Council of Negro Women, is located on Pennsylvania Avenue in Washington DC. In 2004, Height was recognized by Barnard for her achievements as an honorary alumna during the fiftieth anniversary of the *Brown vs. Board of Education* decision.

In 2005, the musical stage play *If This Hat Could Talk*, based on her memoir, *Open Wide the Freedom Gates*, debuted. It showcased her unique perspectives on the civil rights movement and detailed many of the behind-the-scenes figures and mentors who shaped her life, including Mary McLeod Bethune and Eleanor Roosevelt.

Height was the chairperson of the Executive Committee of the Leadership Conference on Organization in the USA. She was an honored guest at the inauguration of President Barack Obama in 2009. She attended the National Black Family Reunion, celebrated on the National Mall in Washington DC, every year until her death in 2010.

HANK AARON

Born: February 5, 1934-

Henry Louis Aaron (nicknamed "Hammer," "Hammering Hank" and "Bad Henry") is an American baseball player whose career spanned the years 1954 through 1976. Aaron is widely considered one of the greatest baseball players of all time. In 1999, editors at the *Sporting News* ranked Aaron fifth on the list of the greatest baseball players. After playing with the Indianapolis Clowns of the Negro American League and in the minor leagues, Aaron started his major league career in 1954.

He played twenty-one seasons with the Milwaukee and Atlanta Braves in the National League, and his last two years (1975–1976) with the Milwaukee Brewers in the American League. His most notable achievement was breaking the career home run record of 714 set by Babe Ruth. During his professional career, Aaron performed at a consistently high level for an extended period of time. He hit twenty-four or more home runs every year from 1955 through 1973, and he is the only player to hit thirty or more home runs in a season at least fifteen times.

Aaron made the All-Star team every year from 1955 until 1975, and he won three Gold Glove awards. In 1957, he won the National League Most Valuable Player award; that same year, the Braves won the World Series for the only time during his career. In 1963, Hank Aaron became the first player to lead the National League in runs, home runs, and runs batted in and sadly not to be nominated after all of this as Most Valuable Player.

Although Aaron himself downplayed the chase to surpass Babe Ruth, baseball enthusiasts and the national media grew increasingly excited as he closed in on the home run record. During the summer of 1973, Aaron received thousands of letters every week; the Braves ended up hiring a secretary to help him sort through it.

On September 29, 1973, Aaron hit home run number 713, and with one day remaining in the season, many expected him to tie the record. But in his final game, playing against the Houston Astros (led by manager Leo Durocher, who had once roomed with Babe Ruth), he was unable to achieve this. After the game, Aaron stated that his only fear was that he might not live to see the 1974 season.

Over the winter, Aaron received a large assortment of hate mail and death threats from people who did not want to see a black man break Ruth's nearly sacrosanct home run record. Babe Ruth's widow, Claire Hodgson, denounced the racism and declared that her husband would have enthusiastically cheered Aaron's attempt at the record.

The threats extended to those who provided positive press coverage of Aaron. Lewis Grizzard, then editor of the *Atlanta Journal*, reported receiving numerous phone calls calling them "nigger lovers" for covering Aaron's chase. While preparing the massive coverage of the home run record, Grizzard quietly prepared an obituary for Aaron, scared that he might be murdered.

Sports Illustrated pointedly summarized the racist vitriol that Aaron was forced to endure:

Is this to be the year in which a man takes on one of the most hallowed individual records in American sports? Or will it be remembered as the season in which Aaron, the most dignified of athletes, was besieged with hate mail and trapped by the cobwebs and goblins that lurk in baseballs attic?

Aaron received an outpouring of public support in response to the bigotry. In August 1973, newspaper cartoonist Charles Schulz satirized the anti-Aaron campaign in a series of *Peanuts* strips in which Snoopy attempts to break Ruth's record, only to be besieged with hate mail. In one strip, Lucy said, "Hank Aaron is a great player ... but you. If you break Babe Ruth's record, it'll be a disgrace."

Coincidentally, Snoopy was only one home run short of tying the record when Charlie Brown got picked off during his last at bat, and as it turned out, Aaron finished the 1973 season one home run short of Ruth. Babe Ruth's widow, Claire Hodgson, even denounced the racism and declared that her husband would have enthusiastically cheered Aaron's attempt at the record.

As the 1974 season began, Aaron's pursuit of the record caused a small controversy. The Braves opened the season on the road in Cincinnati, with a three-game series against the Reds. Braves management wanted him to break the record in Atlanta and wanted Aaron to sit out the first three games. But baseball commissioner Bowie Kuhn ruled that he had to play two games in the first series. He did, and tied Babe Ruth's record in his very first at bat off Reds pitcher Jeff Billingham, but he did not hit another home run in the series.

The team returned to Atlanta, and on April 8, 1974, a record crowd of 53,775 showed up for the. In the fourth inning, Aaron hit home run number 715 off Dodgers pitcher Al Downing. Although outfielder Bill Buckner nearly went over the outfield wall trying to catch it, the ball landed in the Braves bullpen, where relief pitcher Tom House caught it. While cannons were fired in celebrations, two white college students, Cliff Courtney and Britt Gaston, sprinted onto the field and jogged alongside Aaron for part of his circuit around the bases, temporarily startling him. As the fans cheered wildly, Aaron's parents ran onto the field as well.

Dodger's broadcaster Vin Scully addressed the racial tension in his call of the home run: "What a marvelous moment for baseball; what a marvelous moment for Atlanta and the state of Georgia; what a marvelous moment for the country and the world. A black man is getting a standing ovation in the Deep South for breaking a record of an all-time baseball idol … and it is great for all of us, and particularly for Henry Aaron … and for the first time in a long time, that poker face in Aaron shows the tremendous strain and relief over what it must have been like to live for the past several months."

Aaron's consistency helped him to establish a number of important hitting records during his twenty-three-year career. Aaron holds the MLB record for the most career runs batted in (2,297) and the most career extra-base hits (1,477). Aaron is also in the top five for career hits with 3,771 (third) and runs with 2,174 (tied for fourth with Babe Ruth). He is one of only four players to have at least seventeen seasons with 150 or more hits. He also is in second place in home runs 755 and at bats (12,364), and in third place in games played (3,298).

JACK ROOSEVELT "JACKIE" ROBINSON

Born: January 31, 1919

Died: October 24, 1972

Robinson was the first black major league baseball player of the modern era. Robinson broke the baseball color line when he debuted with the

Brooklyn Dodgers in 1947. As the first black man to play in the major leagues, he was instrumental in bringing racial segregation to professional baseball, which had relegated black players to the Negro Leagues for six decades. The example of his character and unquestionable talent challenged the traditional bases of segregation, which then marked many other aspects of American life, and contributed greatly to the civil rights movement.

In addition to his cultural impact, Robinson had an exceptional baseball career. Over ten seasons, he played in six World Series and contributed to the Dodgers' 1955 World Championship. He was selected for six consecutive All Star Games from 1949 to 1954, was the recipient of the inaugural MLB Rookie of the Year award in 1947, and won the National League Most Valuable Player award in 1949 (the first black player so honored). Robinson was inducted into the Baseball Hall of Fame in 1962. In 1997, Major League Baseball retired his uniform number, 42, from all major league teams.

Robinson was also known for his pursuits outside the baseball diamond. He was the first black television baseball analyst and the first black vice president of a major American corporation. In the 1960s, he helped establish the Freedom National Bank, an African American–owned financial institution based in Harlem. In recognition of his achievements on and off the field, Robinson was posthumously awarded the Presidential Medal of Freedom and the Congressional Gold Medal.

Early Life

Robinson was born into a family of sharecroppers in Cairo, Georgia. He was the youngest of five children, after siblings Edgar, Frank, Matthew, and Willa Mae. After Robinson's father left the family in 1920, they moved to Pasadena, California. The extended Robinson family grew up in relative poverty in an otherwise affluent community; Robinson and his minority friends were excluded from many recreational opportunities.

In 1942, Robinson was drafted and assigned to a segregated Army cavalry unit in Fort Riley, Kansas. Having the requisite qualifications, Robinson and several other black soldiers applied for admission to an Officer Candidate School (OCS) in Fort Riley. Practically speaking, few black applicants were admitted into OCS. Robinson's application was delayed for several months. After protests by heavyweight boxing champion Joe Louis (then stationed in Fort Riley) and the help of Truman K. Gibson (then an assistant civilian aid to the secretary of war), the men were accepted into OCS. This military experience spawned a personal friendship between Robinson and Louis. Upon finishing OCS, Robinson was commissioned a second lieutenant in January 1943.

An event on July 6, 1944, derailed Robinson's military career. While awaiting results of hospital tests on the ankle he had injured in junior college, Robinson boarded an Army bus with a fellow officer's wife. The bus driver ordered Robinson to move to the back of the bus. Robinson refused. The driver backed down, but after reaching the end of the line, he summoned the military police, who took Robinson into custody. When Robinson later confronted the investigating duty officer about racist questioning, the officer recommended that Robinson be court-martialed. Robinson's commander refused to authorize legal action, and Robinson was transferred to the 758th Battalion, where the command quickly consented to charge Robinson with multiple offenses including public drunkenness, even though Robinson did not drink.

By the time of the court-martial in August 1944, the charges against Robinson had been reduced to two counts of insubordination during questioning. Robinson was acquitted by an all-white panel of nine officers. His black tank unit saw combat in World War II.

Robinson received an honorable discharge in November 1944. Robinson met a former player for the Kansas City Monarchs of the Negro American League, who encouraged him to write the Monarchs and ask for a tryout. Robinson soon wore the uniform of the Kansas City Monarchs. During the season, Robinson pursued potential major-league interest. The Boston Red Sox held a tryout at Fenway Park for Robinson and other black players on April 16. The tryout, however, was a farce, chiefly designed to assuage the desegregationist sensibilities of powerful Boston City Councilman Isadore Muchonick. Even with the stands limited to management, Robinson left the tryout humiliated, and more than fourteen years later, the Red Sox became the last major league team to integrate its roster.

In 1946, Robinson arrived at Daytona Beach, Florida, for spring training with the Montréal Royals, a Class AAA team, the highest level of minor league baseball. Robinson's presence was a controversy in racially charged Florida. He was not allowed to stay with his teammates at the team hotel, so he lodged instead at the home of a local black politician. In Sanford, Florida, the police chief threatened to cancel games if Robinson played; as a result, Robinson was sent back to Daytona Beach. In Jacksonville, the stadium was padlocked shut without warning on game day by order of the city's parks and public property director.

Robinson made his Royals debut on March 17, 1946, in an exhibition game against the Dodgers. The following year, six days before the start of the 1947 season, the Dodgers called Robinson up to the major leagues. With Eddie Stanky entrenched at second base for the Dodgers, Robinson played his initial major league season as a first baseman. On April 15, 1947, Robinson made his major league debut at Ebbets Field before a crowd of 26,623 spectators, including more than 14,000 black patrons. Black fans began flocking to see the Dodgers when they came to town, abandoning their Negro League teams.

During the 1951 season, Robinson led the National League in double plays and kept the Dodgers in contention for the pennant.

During the last game of the season, in the thirteenth inning, he had a hit to tie the game and then he won the game with a home run in the fourteenth. This forced a playoff against the New York Giants, which the Dodgers lost.

Robinson was named by *Time* magazine as one of the one hundred most influential people in the twentieth century.

Robinson was also honored by the USPS on three separate postage stamps in 1982, 1999, and 2000.

Mahalia Jackson

Born: October 26, 1911

Died: January 27, 1972

Jackson was an African American gospel singer. Possessing a powerful contralto voice, she was referred to as "the Queen of Gospel." Jackson became one of the most influential gospel singers in the world and was heralded internationally as a singer and civil rights activist; entertainer Harry Belafonte called her "the single most powerful black woman in the United States."

She recorded about thirty albums (mostly for Columbia Records) during her career, and her records included a dozen million-sellers.

1950 through 1970

In 1950, she became the first gospel singer to perform in New York's Carnegie Hall when Joe Bostic produced the Negro Gospel and Religious Music Festival. She started touring Europe in 1952 and was hailed by critics as the "World's Greatest Gospel Singer." In Paris she was called "the Angel of Peace," and throughout the continent she sang to capacity audiences. The tour, however, had to be cut short due to exhaustion. Jackson began a radio series on CBS and signed to Columbia Records in 1954.

On November 17, 1954, *Downbeat* magazine said, "It is generally agreed that the greatest spiritual singer now alive is Mahalia Jackson." Her debut album for Columbia was *The World's Greatest Gospel Singer*, recorded in 1954, followed by a Christmas album called *Sweet Little Jesus Boy* and *Bless This House* in 1956.

Mahalia Jackson died in Chicago of heart failure and diabetes complications. Two cities paid tribute, Chicago and New Orleans. Beginning in Chicago, outside the greater Salem Baptist Church, fifty thousand people filed silently past her mahogany glass-topped coffin. The next day, six thousand people filled every seat and stood along the walls of the city's public concert hall, the Arie Crown Theater of McCormick Place, for the two-hour funeral service.

Mahalia's pastor, the Rev. Leon Jenkins, Mayor Richard J Daley, and Coretta Scott King eulogized Mahalia during the Chicago funeral as "a friend, proud, black, and beautiful."

Sammy Davis Jr. and Ella Fitzgerald paid their respects. Dr. Joseph H. Jackson, president of the National Baptist Convention, delivered the eulogy at the Chicago funeral. Aretha Franklin closed the Chicago rites with a moving rendition of "Precious Lord, Take My Hand."

BILL COSBY

Born: July 12, 1937-

Spouse: Camille Hanks (1964–present)

William Henry Cosby Jr. is an American comedian, actor, author, television producer, educator, musician, and activist. A veteran standup performer, he got his start in various clubs and then landed a starring role in the 1960s action show, *I Spy*. He later starred in his own series, *The Cosby Show*.

He was one of the major characters on the children's television series *The Electric Company*, and he created the educational cartoon comedy series *Fat Albert and the Cosby Kids*, about a group of young friends growing up in the city. Cosby has also acted in a number of films.

During the 1980s, Cosby produced and starred in what is considered to be one of the decade's defining sitcoms, *The Cosby Show*, which aired from 1984 to 1992. The sitcom highlighted the African American family. He also produced a spinoff sitcom, *A Different World*, which became second to *The Cosby Show* in ratings. He starred in *Kids Say the Darndest Things* for two seasons.

He has been a sought after spokesman and has endorsed a number of products including Jell-O, Kodak film, Ford, Texas Instruments, and Coca-Cola. In 1976, Cosby earned a doctorate of education degree from the University of Massachusetts. For his doctorate research, he wrote a dissertation entitled, "An Integration of the Visual Media via Fat Albert and the Cosby Kids," which was utilized in elementary school curriculum as a teaching aid and vehicle to achieve increased learning. In 2002, scholar Molefi Kete Asante included him in his book, *The 100 Greatest African Americans*.

SIDNEY POITIER

Born: February 20, 1927-

Poitier is a Bahamian American actor, film director, author, and diplomat. In 1963, he became the first black man to win an Academy Award for best actor for his role in *Lilies of the Field*. The significance of this achievement was later bolstered in 1967, when he starred in three well-received films, *To Sir with Love, In the Heat of the Night*, and *Guess Who's Coming to Dinner*, making him the top box office star of that year. In 1999, the American Film Institute named Poitier among the greatest male stars of all time, ranking twenty-second on the list of twenty-five.

Poitier has directed a number of popular movies such as *A Piece of the Action, Uptown Saturday Night* and *Let's Do It Again* (with friend

Bill Cosby), and *Stir Crazy* (starring Richard Pryor and Gene Wilder). In 2002, thirty-eight years after receiving the Best Actor award, Poitier was chosen by the Academy of Motion Picture Arts and Sciences to receive an honorary award: "To Sidney Poitier, in recognition of his remarkable accomplishments as an artist and as a human being." Since 1997 he has been the Bahamian ambassador to Japan. On August 12, 2009, Poitier was awarded the Presidential Medal of Freedom, America's highest civilian honor, by President Barack Obama.

Poitier was married to Juanita Hardy from 1950 until 1965. He married Joanna Shimkus, a Canadian-born actress, on January 23, 1976. He has four daughters with his first wife and two with his second.

In 1944, Poitier joined the American Negro Theater but was rejected by audiences. Contrary to what was expected of black actors at the time, Poitier was tone deaf and unable to sing.

Determined to refine his act and to rid himself of his noticeable Bahamian accent, he spent the next six months dedicating himself to achieve theater success. On his second attempt at the theater, he was given a leading role in a Broadway production, *Lysistrata*, for which he received good reviews. By the end of 1949, he had to choose between leading roles on stage and in movies. Poitier's breakout role was as a member of an incorrigible high school class in *Blackboard Jungle*.

In 1958, Poitier became the first black actor to be nominated for an Academy Award for *The Defiant Ones*. He was also the first black actor to win the Academy Award for Best Actor (for *Lilies of the Field* in 1963).

JOSEPHINE BAKER

Born: Freda Josephine McDonald 1906, St. Louis, Missouri

Died 1975 (age 68) in Paris, France

Genres: Cabaret, music hall, French pop, French jazz, dancer, singer, actress, vocalist

JOSEPHINE BAKER WAS THE first African American female to star in a major motion picture; she also integrated an American concert hall. In 1963, Baker was by the side of Dr. Martin Luther King Jr. during the

March on Washington. After his assassination, she was asked by Coretta Scott King to lead the civil rights movement. Baker often faced racism in show business because of her color. Yet she continued through this evil hatred that held America bound in its darkness.

HARRY BELAFONTE

Born: March 1, 1927-

Harold George "Harry" Belafonte is an American singer, songwriter, actor, and social activist. He was dubbed the "King of Calypso" for popularizing the Caribbean musical style for an international audience in the 1950s.

Belafonte is perhaps best known for singing "The Banana Boat Song," with its signature lyric "Day-O." Throughout his career, he has been an advocate for civil rights and humanitarian causes and was a vocal critic of the policies of the George W. Bush administration. From the mid-1970s to early 1980s he spent the greater part of his time touring Japan, Europe, and Cuba.

His involvement in USA for Africa during the mid-1980s resulted in renewed interest in his music, culminating in a record deal with EMI. In 1988, he released his first album of original material in over a decade, *Paradise in Gazankulu*. The album contains ten protest songs against South Africa's apartheid policy. In the same year Belafonte, as UNICEF goodwill ambassador attended a symposium in Harare, Zimbabwe, to focus attention on child survival and development in southern African countries. As part of the symposium, he performed a concert for UNICEF.

In 1050, Belafonte became the first African American to win an Emmy, for his solo TV special entitled *Tonight with Belafonte*. During the 1960s he appeared on TV specials alongside such artists as Julie Andrews, Petula Clark, Nina Warren, and Nana Mouskouri. In 1978, he was a guest star on a memorable episode of *The Muppet Show*, on which he performed "The Banana Boat Song." The episode is best known for Belafonte's rendition of the spiritual song, "Turn the World Around," which he performed with Muppets wearing African tribal masks.

It became one of the series' most famous performances. It was reportedly Jim Henson's favorite episode, and Belafonte reprised the song at Henson's memorial in 1990. "Turn the World Around" was also included in the 2005 official hymnal supplement of the Unitarian Universalist Association, *Singing the Journey.* Belafonte received Kennedy Center Honors in 1989. He was awarded the National Medal of Arts in 1994 and won a Grammy Lifetime Achievement Award in 2000. His last concert was a benefit concert for the Atlanta Opera on October 25, 2003. In a 2007 interview he stated that he had since retired from performing. Belafonte supported the civil rights movement in the 1950s and was one of Martin Luther King Jr.'s confidants.

He provided for King's family, since King made only $8,000 a year as a preacher. Like many civil rights activists, Belafonte was blacklisted during the McCarthy era. He bailed King out of the Birmingham City Jail and raised thousands of dollars to release other civil rights protesters. He financed the Freedom Rides, supported voter registration drives, and helped to organize the March on Washington in 1963. In 1985, he helped organize the Grammy Award–winning song "We Are the World," a multiartist effort to raise funds for Africa.

He performed in the Live Aid concert that same year. In 1987, he received an appointment to UNICEF as a goodwill ambassador. Following his appointment, Belafonte traveled to Dakar, Senegal, where he served as chairman of the International Symposium of Artists and Intellectuals for African Children. He also helped to raise funds alongside more than twenty artists in the largest concert ever held in sub-Saharan Africa. In 1994, he went on a mission to Rwanda and launched a media campaign to raise awareness of the needs of the Rwandan children.

In 2001, he went to South Africa to support the campaign against HIV/AIDS. In 2002, Africare awarded him the Bishop John T. Walker Distinguished Humanitarian Service Award for his efforts to assist Africa.

In 2004, Belafonte went to Kenya to promote the importance of educating children in the region. Belafonte has been involved in prostate cancer advocacy since 1996, when he was diagnosed and successfully treated for the disease. On June 27, 2006, Belafonte was the recipient of the BET Humanitarian Award. In 2006, he was named one of nine Impact Award recipients by *AARP Magazine.*

Opposition to the George W. Bush Administration
In 2002, Belafonte achieved widespread attention for his political views when he began making a series of comments about President George W. Bush and the Iraq War. During a radio interview, Belafonte referred to a quote by Malcolm X when he said, "There is an old saying in the days of slavery. There were those slaves who lived on the plantation and there were those slaves who live in the house. You got the privilege of living in the house if you serve the master, do things exactly the way the master intended to have you serve him. That gave you privilege. Colin Powell is committed to come into the house of the master, as long as he would serve the master, according to the master's purpose. And when Colin Powell dares to suggest something other than what the master wants to hear, he will be turned back out to pasture. And you don't hear much from those who live in the pasture."

Belafonte used the quote to characterize former US Secretaries of State Colin Powell and Condoleezza Rice, both African Americans. Powell and Rice both responded, with Powell calling the remarks "unfortunate" and Rice saying, "I don't need Harry Belafonte to tell me what it means to be black."

LENA HORNE

Born: June 30, 1917

Died May 9, 2010

Lena Mary Calhoun Horne was an American singer, civil rights activist, and dancer. Horne joined the chorus of the Cotton Club at the age of sixteen and became a nightclub performer before moving to Hollywood, where she had small parts in numerous movies and more substantial parts in the films *Cabin in the Sky* and *Stormy Weather*. Due to the Red scare and her left-leaning political views, Horne found herself blacklisted and unable to get work in Hollywood.

Horne returned to her roots as a nightclub performer and then took part in the March on Washington in August 1963. She continued to work as a performer, both in nightclubs and on television, while releasing her well-received record albums. She announced her retirement in March 1980 but the next year starred in a one-woman show, *Lena*

Horne: The Lady and Her Music, which ran for more than three hundred performances on Broadway and earned her numerous awards and accolades. She continued recording and performing sporadically into the 1990s, disappearing from the public eye in 2000.

Horne was born in the Bedford Stuyvesant neighborhood of New York City. Reported to be descended from John Calhoun, both sides of her family were a mixture of African Americans, native Americans (notably Blackfoot), and European Americans, and they belonged to what W. E. du Bois called the Talented 10th, the upper stratum of the middle class, well-educated African Americans.

Her mother, Edna Louise Scottron (1895–1985), daughter of inventor Samuel R. Scottron, was an actress with a black theater troupe and traveled extensively. Scottron's maternal grandmother, Amelie Lewis Ashton, was a Senegalese slave. The young Horne was mainly raised by her grandparents, Cora Calhoun and Edwin Horne.

When Horne was five, she was sent to live in Georgia. For several years, she traveled with her mother. From 1927 to 1929, she lived with her uncle, Frank S. Horan, who was the dean of students at Fort Valley Junior Industrial Institute in Fort Valley, Georgia, and who would later become an advisor to Franklin Delano Roosevelt. From Fort Valley, southwest of Macon, Horne briefly moved to Atlanta with her mother; they returned to New York when Horne was twelve years old.

At the age of eighteen, she moved in with her estranged father in Pittsburgh, staying in the city's Little Harlem for almost five years and learning from native Pittsburghers Billy Strayhorn and Billy Eckstine, as well as other jazz greats. A series of photographs by legendary African American and *Pittsburgh Courier* photographer Teenie Harris captured her youth.

After leaving Hollywood, Horne established herself as one of the premier nightclub performers of the postwar era. She headlined at clubs and hotels throughout the United States, Canada, and Europe, including the Sands Hotel in Las Vegas, the Coconut Grove in Los Angeles, and the Waldorf Astoria in New York. In 1957, a live album entitled *Lena Horne at the Waldorf Astoria* became the biggest selling record by a female artist in the history of the RCA Victor label. In 1958, Horne was nominated for a Tony Award for best actress in a musical (for her part in the calypso musical *Jamaica*).

In 1965, Horne performed on *The Bell Telephone Hour*. From the late 1950s through the 1960s, Horne was a staple of TV variety shows, appearing multiple times on *Perry Como's Kraft Music Hall*, *The Ed Sullivan Show*, and *The Dean Martin Show*. Other programs she appeared on included *The Judy Garland Show*, *The Hollywood Palace*, and *The Andy Williams Show*. Besides two television specials for the BBC (later syndicated in the United States), Horne starred in her own television special in 1969, *Monsanto Night Presents Lena Horne*.

In 1970, she costarred with Harry Belafonte in an hour-long show for ABC; in 1973, she costarred with Tony Bennett. Horne and Bennett subsequently toured the United States and the UK together. In 1976, in "America Salutes Richard Rodgers," she sang a lengthy medley of Rodgers songs with Peggy Lee and Vic Damone. Horne also made several appearances on *The Flip Wilson Show*.

Civil Rights Activism
Horne was long involved with the civil rights movement. In 1941, she sang at Café Society and worked with Paul Robeson. During World War II, when entertaining the troops for the United Service Organizations (USO), she refused to perform for segregated audiences or for groups in which German POWs were seated in front of African American servicemen, according to her Kennedy Center biography. Because the US Army refused to allow integrated audiences, she would put on a show for a mixed audience of black US soldiers and white German POWs.

This bitter disdain of racial hatred from white America surfaced during the concert. Black soldiers were forced to sit *behind* the German POW soldiers. So the great Lena Horne went right on with her show, but instead of performing onstage in front of the German POWs, she left the stage and performed her show *between* the Germans and in front of the black American soldiers.

Thank you, Ms. Horne. After all of the horrible acts forced on our people (e.g., slavery, rape, murder, Jim Crow laws, and hatred), this failed stage antic angered me more than ever. I ask that God will remove this anger from my soul. This despicable act of disrespect and hatred was so unjust against black American soldiers. Even though the soldiers were fighting and dying for their beloved country, white America's heart still displayed hatred even overseas.

Horne appeared at a rally with Medger Evers in Jackson, Mississippi, the weekend before Evers was assassinated. She also met President John F. Kennedy at the White House two days before he was assassinated. She was at the March on Washington and spoke on behalf of the National Association for the Advancement of Colored People (NAACP), SNCC, and the National Council of Negro Women. She also worked with Eleanor Roosevelt to pass antilynching laws. She was a member of Delta Sigma Theta sorority.

Tom Lehrer mentions her in his song, "National Brotherhood Week," in the line "Lena Horne and Sheriff Clark are dancing cheek to cheek" referring (wryly) to Sheriff Jim Clark of Selma, who was responsible for a violent attack on civil rights marchers in 1965.

In her as-told-to autobiography *Lena* by Richard Schickel, Horne recounts the enormous pressures she and Lenny Hayton faced as an interracial couple. In May 1980, she admitted in an *Ebony* interview that she had married Hayton to advance her career and cross the color line in show business, but she learned to love him in a way.

Screenwriter Jenny Lumet, known for her award-winning screenplay *Rachel Getting Married,* is Horne's granddaughter, the daughter of filmmaker Sidney Lumet and Horne's daughter Gail. Horne's other grandchildren include Amy Lumet and her son's three children, Thomas, William, and Lena.

Legacy

In 2003, ABC announced that Janet Jackson would star as Horne in a television biopic. Following Jackson's wardrobe malfunction debacle during the 2004 Super Bowl, however, *Variety* reported that Horne demanded that Jackson be dropped from the project. ABC executives resisted Horne's demand, according to the Associated Press report, but Jackson representatives told the trade newspaper that she left willingly after Horne asked that she not take part. Oprah Winfrey told Alicia Keys during a 2005 interview on *The Oprah Winfrey Show* that she was considering producing the biopic and casting Keys as Horne.

PAUL MOONEY

Born: August 4, 1941-

Paul Mooney is an American comedian, writer, social critic, and television and film actor. He was also featured on one of Tru TV's reality shows, *Ma's Roadhouse*.

While Mooney was ringmaster with the Gatti-Charles Circus, he always found himself writing comedy and telling jokes, which would later help him land his first professional work as a writer for Richard Pryor.

Mooney wrote some of Pryor's routine for his appearance on *Saturday Night Live* and co-wrote his material for *Live on the Sunset Strip, Bicentennial Nigger*, and *Jo Jo Dancer, Your Life Is Calling*. As the head writer for *The Richard Pryor Show*, he gave many young standup comics, such as Robin Williams, Marsha Warfield, John Witherspoon, and Tim Reid, their first break in show business.

Mooney also wrote for Redd Foxx's *Sanford and Son* and *Good Times*; acted in several cult classics including *Which Way Is Up, Bustin' Loose*, and *Hollywood Shuffle*; and portrayed singer/songwriter Sam Cooke in *The Buddy Holly Story*.

He was the head writer for the first year of *In Living Color*, creating the character Homey D. Clown, played by Damon Wayans. Mooney later went on to play Junebug, Wayans' father in the Spike Lee film *Bamboozled*. Much of Mooney's material is based on racism in the United States, which disturbs some audience members. Such incidents can be seen in movies, heard on comedy albums like *Race* and *Master Piece*, and seen in his DVD *Know Your History: Jesus Is Black; So Was Cleopatra*.

On November 26, 2006, Mooney appeared on CNN and talked about how he would stop using the word "nigga" due to Michael Richards's outburst on stage at the Laugh Factory. He referred to Richards as having become his "Dr. Phil," curing him of the use of the epithet. Mooney also said, "We're gonna stop using the n-word. I'm gonna stop using it. I'm not going to use it again and I'm not gonna use the b-word. And we're going to put an end to the n-word. Just say no to the n-word. We want all human beings throughout the world to stop using the n-word."

On November 30, he elaborated upon these remarks as a guest on the National Public Radio program *News and Notes*. He declared that he would convene a conference on this controversial subject in the near future, as well as perform his first "n-word-free" comedy in the upcoming days.

The show took place at the Lincoln Theater, following a set by Dick Gregory, on December 2, 2006. Mooney almost made it through his entire set, about an hour of jokes, before he mistakenly used the word in a routine on O. J. Simpson. He ran offstage, covering his face in his hands, and walked back on a few moments later, saying, "I'm really going to get it now. This is probably already on the Internet."

On the BET special *25 Events that Mis-Shaped Black America*, Mooney repeated that he would no longer use the word. He was quoted as saying, "Instead of saying 'What's up, my nigga,' say 'What's up, my Michael Richards.'" At a summit with Jesse Jackson, Rev. Al Sharpton, and Richards, Mooney forgave Richards.

AL SHARPTON

Born: October 3, 1954-

Alfred Charles Sharpton Jr. is an American Baptist minister, civil rights activist, and television/radio talk show host. In 2004, he was a candidate for the Democratic nomination for the US presidential election. He hosts his own radio talk show, *Keepin It Real*, and he makes regular guest appearances on Fox News, CNN, and MSNBC. He was named the host of MSNBC's *Politics Nation*, a nightly talk show, which premiered on August 29, 2011.

Sharpton's supporters praise "his ability and willingness to deny the power structure that is seen as the cause of their suffering and consider him a man who is willing to tell it like it is." Former New York Mayor Ed Koch, a one-time foe, said that Sharpton deserves the respect he enjoys among African Americans: he is willing to go to jail for them, and he is there when they need him. His critics describe him as "a political radical who is to blame for the deterioration of race relations." Sociologist Orlando Patterson has referred to him as a racial arsonist, while liberal columnist Derek C. Jackson has called him the black equivalent of Richard Nixon and Pat Robertson. Sharpton sees much of the criticism as a sign of his effectiveness.

"In many ways, what they consider criticism is complimenting my job," he said. "An activist's job is to make public rights issues until there can be a climate for change."

Al Sharpton Jr. was born in the Brownfield neighborhood of Brooklyn, New York. He preached his first sermon at the age of four and worked with gospel singer Mahalia Jackson.

Sharpton graduated from Samuel J. Tilden High School in Brooklyn and attended Brooklyn College, dropping out after two years in 1975. He became a tour manager for James Brown in 1971. In 1971, while touring with James Brown, he met his future wife, Kathy Jordan, who was a backup singer. Sharpton and Jordan married in 1980 and separated in 2004.

In 1969, Sharpton was appointed by Jesse Jackson as a youth director of Operation Breadbasket, a group that focused on the promotion of new and better jobs for African Americans. In 1971, Sharpton founded the National Youth Movement to raise resources for impoverished youth.

In September 2007, when he was asked whether he thought it was important for the United States to have a black president, Sharpton said, "It will be a great moment as long as the black candidate was supporting the interest that would inevitably help our people. A lot of my friends went with Clarence Thomas and regretted it to this day. I don't assume that just because somebody's my color, they are my kind. I'm warming up to Obama, but I'm not there yet."

At the age of nine, Sharpton was ordained a Pentecostal minister; in the late 1980s Sharpton became a Baptist. He was rebaptized as a member of the Bethany Baptist Church in 1994 by the Rev. William Jones and became a Baptist minister.

In June 2005, Sharpton signed with Radio One to host a daily national talk radio program; *Keepin It Real with Al Sharpton* began airing on January 30, 2006. In addition, since June 29, 2011, Sharpton has become a regular guest host for MSNBC's *The Ed Show*, filling in for host Ed Schultz.

Tom Joyner

Born: November 23, 1949-

Thomas Joyner is host of the nationally syndicated *Tom Joyner Morning Show* and founder of Reach Media, the Tom Joyner Foundation, and BlackAmericaweb.com.

He began his broadcasting career in Montgomery, Alabama, and worked at a number of radio stations in the South before moving to Chicago.

In the mid-1980s, Joyner was simultaneously offered two positions: a morning show in Dallas and an afternoon show in Chicago. Instead of choosing between the two, Joyner chose to take both jobs, and for years he commuted daily by plane between the two cities, earning the nicknames "the Fly Jock" and "the hardest working man in radio."

He later told *Radio Inc.* magazine that he racked up seven million frequent flyer miles over the course of his employment at both stations.

In 1994, Joyner was signed by ABC Radio Networks to host a nationally syndicated program, *The Tom Joyner Morning Show*, featuring Joyner and a team of comedians and commentators discussing the latest news and sports of the day, and playing popular R&B hits.

Joyner has been an advocate for voter registration and often promotes voter registration over the air and on his website. Joyner also raises awareness regarding Alzheimer's; he participated in the 2011 Alzheimer's Association walk to end Alzheimer's.

Joyner also founded the Tom Joyner Foundation to provide financial assistance to students at historically black colleges and universities. Since 1998, it has raised more than $55 million. The Tom Joyner Foundation also hosts an annual fundraising cruise.

On October 7, 2004, Joyner was awarded the NAB Marconi Radio Award. On January 12, 2008, Joyner was inducted in the International Civil Rights Walk of Fame at the Martin Luther King Jr. National Historic Site.

JOE MADISON

Born: 1949-

Joe Madison, also known as "the Black Eagle," is an American radio talk show host and activist. Madison has managed to trace his origins back to Sierra Leon and Mozambique.

Madison was born in Dayton, Ohio, and received a Bachelor of Arts degree from Washington University in St. Louis. During college he was an all-conference running back and baritone soloist with the university's concert chorus. Madison spent his young adulthood in various positions in the NAACP and was elected executive director of Detroit's NAACP branch at the age of twenty-four. He is the youngest person to be appointed to the position.

In addition to his broadcast, Madison has engaged in hunger strikes and other activism ranging from Sudanese slavery to securing a star for the Four Tops on the Hollywood Walk of Fame. On August 27, 2010, he had a confrontation on his radio show with Glenn Beck about the August 28th Restoring Honor Rally. Madison did not physically attack Beck, but Fox sources said there was a racial implication to the argument.

Madison lives in Washington DC with his wife, Sherry.

My personal opinion is that Joe Madison is the best dressed man on radio and television.

CAB CALLOWAY

Born Cabell Calloway III, December 25, 1907, Rochester, New York

Died November 18, 1994

Calloway, jazz and blues musician, bandleader, singer-songwriter was a master of energetic scat singing; he had one of the most popular African American big bands from the start of the 1930s through the late 1940s. Calloway's band featured trumpeters Dizzy Gillespie and Doc Cheatham, saxophonist Ben Webster and Leon Chu Berry, New Orleans guitar ace Danny Barker, and bassist Milt Hinton. Calloway continued to perform until his death in 1994. His band was one of the most popular American jazz bands of the 1930s. After the 1942–1944 musicians' strike ended, he continued to record prolifically.

Calloway's vocal style is a blend of hot scat singing and improvisation, coupled with a very traditional vaudeville singing style.

DICK GREGORY

Born: October 12, 1932-

St. Louis, Missouri

Spouse: Lillian Gregory (1959–present); ten children

Notable works and roles: *In Living Black* and *White Nigger*

Autobiography: *Write Me In*

Richard Claxton "Dick" Gregory is an American comedian, social activist, social critic, writer, and entrepreneur.

Gregory is an influential American comic who used his performance skills to convey to both white and black audiences his political message on civil rights. His social satire changed the way white Americans perceive African American comedians. Influenced to stand up for civil rights by his early environment of poverty, Gregory was one of the first comedians to successfully perform for both black and white audiences.

Gregory met his wife Lillian at an African American club; they married in 1959. They had ten children total. In 1973, the Gregory family moved to Plymouth, Massachusetts, where he developed an interest in vegetarianism. Gregory was active in the civil rights movement, and on October 7, 1963, he spoke in Selma, Alabama, two days before the voter registration drive known as "Freedom Day."

In 1964, he became more involved in struggles for civil rights, activism against the Vietnam War, economic reform, antidrug issues, and conspiracy theories. As a part of his activism, he went on several hunger strikes.

In 1967, Gregory began his political career by running against

Richard J. Daley for mayor of Chicago. Though he did not emerge victorious, this would not prove to be the end of Gregory's dalliances with electoral politics.

Gregory unsuccessfully ran for president of the United States in 1968, as a write-in candidate of the Freedom and Peace Party, which had broken off from the Peace and Freedom Party. He won 47,097 votes (including one from Hunter S. Thompson), with fellow activist Mark Lane as his running mate. His efforts landed him on the master list of Nixon political opponents.

He then wrote the book *Write Me In* about his presidential campaign. One interesting anecdote in the book concerned a publicity stunt in which Operation Breadbasket in Chicago printed one dollar bills with Gregory's image on them. Some of these bills made it into circulation in cash transactions, causing considerable problems, but priceless publicity.

Gregory avoided being charged with a federal crime, later joking that the bills couldn't really be considered US currency because "everyone knows a black man will never be on a US bill."

Shortly after this, Gregory became an outspoken critic of the Warren Commission, which concluded that President Kennedy was assassinated by Lee Harvey Oswald. On March 6, 1975, Gregory and assassination researcher Robert Groden appeared on Geraldo Rivera's late-night ABC talk show *Good Night America*. That night, the famous Zapruder film of JFK's assassination was shown to the public; response and outrage to that showing led to the forming of the Hort-Schweiker investigation, which contributed to the Church Committee Investigation on Intelligence Activities by the United States, which resulted in an investigation by the House Select Committee on Assassination.

Gregory was an outspoken feminist activist, and on August 26, 1978, he joined Gloria Steinem, Betty Friedan, Bella Abzug, Margaret Heckler, and Barbara Mikulski to lead the National ERA March for Ratification and Extension down Washington's Pennsylvania Avenue. Over one hundred thousand people demonstrated to extend the ratification deadline for the proposed Equal Rights Amendment to the Constitution. The march was ultimately successful in extending the deadline to June 30, 1982, and Gregory joined other activists in the Senate for celebrations and victory speeches by pro-ERA Senators,

Representatives, and activists. The ERA narrowly failed to be ratified by the extended ratification date, but the women's movement was largely successful in securing gender equality in the laws and society.

On July 21, 1979, Gregory appeared at the Amanala Festival, blaming President Carter and showing his support for the international antiapartheid movements. Gregory and Mark Lane demanded more research into the assassinations of Dr. Martin Luther King Jr., which helped move the US House Assassinations Committee to investigate the murder. The pair wrote the book *Code Name Zorro*, which postulated that convicted assassin James Earl Ray did not act alone. Gregory has also argued that the moon landing was faked and the commonly accepted account of the 9/11 attacks is wrong, among other conspiracy theories.

Gregory was an outspoken activist during the US embassy hostage crisis in Iran. In 1980, he traveled to Tehran to attempt to negotiate the hostages' release and engaged in a public hunger strike there; he weighed less than a hundred pounds when he returned to the United States.

In 1998, Gregory advocated for a raw fruit and vegetable diet. Gregory first became a vegetarian in the 1960s and had lost a considerable amount of weight by going on extreme fasts, some lasting upwards of fifty days. He developed a diet drink called "Bahamian Diet Nutritional Drink" and went on TV shows to help the morbidly obese. In 1988, he helped Walter Hudson, a 1,200-pound Long Island man, drop nearly 600 pounds in only a few months on a liquid diet.

In 2005, at a civil rights rally marking the fortieth anniversary of the Voting Rights Act, Gregory criticized the United States, calling it "the most dishonest, ungodly, unspiritual nation that ever existed in the history of the planet. As we talk now, America is 5 percent of the world's population and consumes 96 percent of world's hard drugs."

HATTIE MCDANIEL

Born: June 10, 1895, Wichita, Kansas

Died: October 26, 1952 (age 57)

Hattie McDaniel was the first African American actress to win an Academy Award. In 1939, she won the award for Best Supporting Actress for her role of Mammy in *Gone with the Wind*.

In addition to acting, McDaniel was a professional singer-songwriter, comedienne, stage actress, radio performer, and television star. She was the first black singer on the radio in America. Over the course of her career, McDaniel appeared in over three hundred films, although she received screen credits for only about eighty. She gained the respect of the African American show business community with her generosity, elegance, and charm. McDaniel has two stars on the Hollywood Walk of Fame, one for her contributions to radio at 6933 Hollywood Boulevard and one for motion pictures at 1719 Vine Street. In 1975, she was inducted into the Black Filmmakers Hall of Fame, and in 2006, she was honored with a US postage stamp.

Early Acting Career
Hattie McDaniel was born to former slaves. She was the youngest of thirteen children. Her father, Henry McDaniel, fought in the Civil War, and her mother, Susan Holbert, was a singer of religious music. In 1900, the family moved to Colorado, living first in Fort Collins and then in Denver, where Hattie graduated from Denver East High School.

Her brother, Sam McDaniel (1886–1962), played the butler in the 1948 Three Stooges short film *Heavenly Days.* Their sister Etta also acted. In addition to performing, Hattie was also a songwriter, a skill she honed while working with her brother's minstrel show. After the death of her brother Otis in 1916, the troupe began to lose money. And it wasn't until 1920 that Hattie received another big opportunity. From 1920 to 1925, she appeared with Professor George Morrison's Melody Hounds, a touring black ensemble, and in the mid-1920s she embarked on a radio career, singing with the Melody Hounds on station KOA in Denver.

When the stock market crashed in 1929, the only work McDaniel could find was as a washroom attendant and waitress at Club Madrid in Milwaukee. Despite the owner's reluctance to let her perform, McDaniel was eventually allowed to take the stage and become a regular.

In 1931, McDaniel made her way to Los Angeles to join Sam, and sisters Etta and Orlena. When she could not get film work, she took jobs as a maid or cook. Sam was working on a radio program called *The Optimistic Do-Nut Hour,* and he was able to get his sister a spot. She appeared on radio as Hi-Hat Hattie, a bossy maid who often forgot her place. The show became extremely popular, but her salary was so low that she had to continue working as a maid. McDaniel befriended several of Hollywood's most popular stars, including Joan Crawford, Tallulah Bankhead, Bette Davis, Shirley Temple, Henry Fonda, Ronald Reagan, Olivia De Havilland, and Clark Gable. She would star with the last two in *Gone with the Wind* (1939).

The competition to play Mammy was almost as stiff as that for Scarlett O'Hara. Eleanor Roosevelt wrote to film producer David O. Selznick to ask that her own maid, Elizabeth McDuffle, be given the part. McDaniel did not think she would be chosen because she was known for being a comic actress. Clark Gable recommended that she get the role, and when she went to her audition dressed in an authentic maid's uniform, she won the part.

In December 1939, the Loew's Grand Theater on Peachtree Street in Atlanta was selected to host the premiere of *Gone with the Wind*. When the date of the premiere approached, all the black actors were told they could not attend and were kept out of the souvenir program. Selznick had attempted to bring Hattie McDaniel, but MGM advised him not to because of Georgia's segregationist laws, which would have required McDaniel to stay in a "blacks only" hotel and prevented her from sitting in the theater with her white peers. Gable angrily threatened to boycott the premiere unless McDaniel was allowed to attend, but she convinced him to attend anyway.

Most of Atlanta's three hundred thousand citizens crowded the route of the seven-mile motorcade that carried the film's other stars and executives from the airport to the Georgian Terrace Hotel, where they stayed. McDaniel was able to attend the Hollywood debut on December 28, 1939. This time, upon Selznick's insistence, her picture was featured prominently in the program (it was also included in programs for all areas outside of the South).

Victory on "Sugar Hill"
Time magazine, December 17, 1945: Spacious, well-kept West Adams Heights still has the complacent look of the days when most of Los Angeles aristocracy lived there. In the Los Angeles courtroom of Judge Thurmond Clarke, some 230 West Adams residents stood at sword points.

Their story was as old as it was ugly. In 1938, Negroes who were able to pay $15,000 and up for Heights property had begun moving into the old eclectic mansions. Many were movie stars like Louise Beavers, Hattie McDaniel, and Ethel Waters. They improved their holdings, kept their well-defined ways, and quickly won more than tolerance from most of their white neighbors. But some whites, refusing to be comforted, had referred to the original racial restriction covenant that came with the development of West Adams Heights back in 1902, which restricted "non-Caucasians" from owning property. For seven years they had tried to enforce it, and then they went to court. Judge Clarke decided to visit the disputed area—popularly known as Sugar Hill—and the next morning he threw the case out of court. His reason: "It is time that members of the Negro race are accorded, without reservations or evasions, the full rights guaranteed them under the Fourteenth Amendment to the federal Constitution."

McDaniel said, "Words cannot express my appreciation." It was McDaniel, the most famous of the black homeowners, who helped to organize the other residents and saved their homes. Loren Miller, a local attorney and publisher of the *California Eagle* newspaper, represented the minority homeowners in their case. McDaniel had purchased her white two-story house in 1942. The house included a large living room, dining room, drawing room, den, butler's pantry, kitchen, service porch, library, and four bedrooms.

Community Service
McDaniel was also a member of Sigma Gamma Rho, an African American sorority States. During World War II, McDaniel chaired the Negro division of the Hollywood Victory Committee, providing entertainment for soldiers stationed at military bases. She also put in numerous personal appearances to hospitals, threw parties, and performed at USO shows and war bond rallies to raise funds to support the war on behalf of the Victory Committee.

Bette Davis also performed for black regiments as the only white member of an acting troupe McDaniel formed; the group also included Lena Horne and Ethel Waters. She was also a member of American Women Voluntary Services.

Death

On October 26, 1952, McDaniel died from breast cancer in in Woodland Hills. She was survived by her brother Sam. Thousands of mourners turned out to remember her life and accomplishments. McDaniel had written about her last wishes: "I desire a white casket and a white shroud; white gardenias in my hair and in my hands, together with a white gardenia and a pillow of red roses. I also wish to be buried in the Hollywood Cemetery."

Hollywood Cemetery on Santa Monica Boulevard was the resting place of movie stars such as Douglas Fairbanks, Rudolph Valentino, and others. The owner, Jules Roth, refused to allow her to be buried there, because they did not take black people. Her second choice was Rosedale Cemetery, where she lies today.

In 1998, Tyler Cassity bought Hollywood Cemetery and renamed it Hollywood Forever Cemetery; he wanted to right the wrong and have McDaniel interred in the cemetery. Her family did not want to disturb her remains after the passage of so much time, and they declined the offer. Hollywood Forever Cemetery instead built a large memorial on the lawn overlooking the lake in honor of McDaniel. It is one of the most popular sites for visitors.

Legacy

In 1975, McDaniel was inducted posthumously into the Black Filmmakers Hall of Fame.

In 1994, actress and singer Karla Burns launched a one-woman show, *Hi-Hat Hattie,* which examined the life of McDaniel. She performed the role in several cities, including off Broadway in New York and Long Beach, California.

In 2002, the legacy of Hattie McDaniel was celebrated when American Movie Classics produced the film *Beyond Touch: The Extraordinary Life of Hattie McDaniel.* The one-hour special showed the struggles and triumphs as McDaniel, in spite of racism and diversity, knocked down the doors of segregation in Hollywood and made her presence known. The film won a Daytime Emmy Award for Outstanding Special.

In 2006, McDaniel was also featured on the Black Heritage Series by the USPS. She was the first black Oscar winner honored with a stamp, which featured a 1941 photograph of McDaniel in the dress she wore when she accepted her Academy Award. In 2009, Mo'Nique won the Oscar as best supporting actress in the film *Precious*; in her acceptance speech, she stated, "I want to thank Ms. Hattie McDaniel for enduring all that she had to so that I would not have to." She wore a blue dress with gardenias in her hair in homage to McDaniel, who had worn the same thing in 1940. Questions arose about whatever became of McDaniel's Oscar. Upon her death, the *Washington Post* reported that the Oscar was donated to Howard University's drama department to be displayed for future generations of students; McDaniel had been honored by the students of Howard University with a luncheon after winning her Oscar.

SAMMY DAVIS JR.

Born: Samuel George Davis Jr., December 8, 1925, Harlem, New York

Died: May 16, 1990 (aged 64) in Beverly Hills, California

Religion: Judaism

Sammy Davis Jr., singer, tap dancer, actor, and musician, was an American entertainer. He was also known for his impersonations of actors and celebrities. Primarily a dancer and singer, Davis started as a child vaudevillian; he became known for his performances on Broadway and in Las Vegas. He went on to become a world-famous recording artist, television actor, and film star. Davis was also a member of Frank Sinatra's "Rat Pack."

At the age of three, Davis began his career in vaudeville with his father and uncle as the Will Mastin Trio. Davis became an overnight sensation following a nightclub performance at Ciro's after the 1951 Academy Awards. He became a recording artist in 1954.

During World War II, the Army assigned Davis to an entertainment special services unit that was integrated, and he found that the spotlight lessened the prejudice. Even prejudiced white men admired and respected his performances. "My talent was the weapon, the power, the way for me to fight. It was the one way I might hope to affect a man's thinking," he said.

In 1959, Davis became a member of the famous Rat Pack, led by his friend Frank Sinatra; the group included fellow performers Dean Martin, Joey Bishop, and Peter Lawford. Initially, Sinatra called the gathering "the Clan," but Sammy voiced his opposition, saying it reminded people of the racist group Ku Klux Klan. Sinatra renamed the group "the Summit," but the media referred to them as "the Rat Pack."

Car Accident and Conversion to Judaism
On November 19, 1954, Davis was in an automobile accident in San Bernardino, California, as he was returning from Las Vegas to Los Angeles. Davis lost his eye as a result of the near-fatal accident; he wore a patch for at least six months. He appeared on *What's My Line* wearing the patch. Later, he was fitted for a glass eye, which he wore for the rest of his life.

While in the hospital, Davis's friend, performer Eddie Cantor, told him about the similarities between the Jewish and black cultures. Prompted by this conversation, Davis, who was born to a Catholic mother and Protestant father, began studying the history of Jews and converted to Judaism. A passage from *A History of the Jews* by Abram L. Sachas, describing the endurance of the Jewish people, intrigued him: "The Jews would not die. Three millennia of prophetic teachings had given them an unwavering spirit of resignation and had created in them a will to live which no disaster could crush." In many ways, the accident marked a turning point in Davis's career, taking him from a well-known entertainer to a national celebrity and icon.

Political Beliefs
Although Davis may have voted Democratic, he felt a lack of respect from the John F Kennedy presidency. He had been removed from the list of performers for Kennedy's inaugural party (hosted by Sinatra) because of Davis's recent interracial marriage to May Britt.

In the early 1970s, Davis supported Republican President Richard M. Nixon (and gave the startled president a hug during a live television broadcast). The incident was controversial, and Davis was given a hostile reception by his peers. Previously Davis had won the respect with his performance as Joe Wellington Jr. in *Golden Boy* and his participation in the civil rights movement.

Unlike Sinatra, Davis voted Democratic for president again after the Nixon administration. He also supported the campaigns of Rev. Jesse Jackson in 1984 and 1988.

Death
Davis died in Beverly Hills of complications from throat cancer. Earlier, when he was told that surgery (laryngectomy) offered him the best chance of survival, Davis replied he would rather keep his voice than have a part of his throat removed; he subsequently was treated with a combination of chemotherapy and radiation. However, a few weeks prior to his death his entire larynx was removed. He was interred in the Forest Lawn Memorial Park Cemetery in Glendale, California, next to his father and Will Mastin.

MARIAN ANDERSON

Born February 27, 1897

Died April 8, 1993

Marion Anderson was one of the most celebrated singers of the twentieth century. Music critic Alan Blyth said, "Her voice was a rich, vibrant contralto of intrinsic beauty." Between 1925 and 1965, she performed in concert and recitals in major music venues and with major orchestras throughout the United States and Europe.

Although she was offered contracts to perform roles with many important European opera companies, Anderson declined, preferring to perform in concert and recital only. She made many recordings that reflected her broad performance repertoire of everything from opera to traditional American songs and spirituals. Anderson became an important figure in the struggle for black artists to overcome racial prejudice in the United States during the middle of the twentieth century. In 1939, the Daughters of the American Revolution refused permission for Anderson to sing to an integrated audience in Constitution Hall. Their race-driven refusal placed Anderson into the spotlight of the international community on a level usually only found by high profile celebrities and politicians.

On Easter Sunday, April 9, 1939, with the aid of President Franklin D. Roosevelt and First Lady Eleanor Roosevelt, Anderson performed a critically acclaimed concert on the steps of the Lincoln Memorial to a crowd of more than seventy-five thousand people and a radio audience in the millions. She continued to break barriers for black artists in the United States, and on January 7, 1955, she became the first black singer to perform at the Metropolitan Opera in New York City.

Her performance as Ulrica in Guiseppe Verdi's *Un Ballo in Maschera* at the Met was the only time she sang in an opera. Anderson was also an important symbol of grace and beauty during the civil rights movement in the 1960s, singing at the March on Washington in 1963. She also worked for several years as a delegate to the United Nations Human Rights Committee and as a goodwill ambassador for the US Department of State.

Anderson was awarded the Presidential Medal of Freedom in 1963, the Kennedy Center Honors in 1978, the National Medal of Arts in 1986, and a Grammy Lifetime Achievement Award in 1991. Throughout her teenage years, Marian remained active in her church's musical activities and then joined the adult choir. She attended Stanton Grammar School, graduating in the summer of 1912. Her family, however, could not afford to send her to high school, nor could they pay for any music lessons. Still, Marian continued to perform whenever she could learn from anyone who was willing to teach her after high school. Marian applied to an all-white music school, the Philadelphia Music Academy (now the University of the Arts) but was turned away because she was black. When she tried to apply, the woman working the admissions counter replied, "We don't take colored." Undaunted, Anderson pursued studies privately with Guiseppe Boghetti and Agnes Reifsnyder with the continued support of the Philadelphia black community.

She met Boghetti through the principal of her high school. Marian auditioned for him by singing "Deep River," and he was immediately brought to tears.

In 1925, Anderson got her first big break when she won first prize in a singing competition sponsored by the New York Philharmonic. As the winner, she got to perform in concert with the orchestra, a performance that scored immediate success with both audience and music critics. Anderson remained in New York to pursue further studies with Frank Laforge. During that time Arthur Judson, whom she had met through the Philharmonic, became her manager.

Over the next several years, she made a number of concert appearances in the United States, but racial prejudice prevented her career from gaining momentum. In 1928, she sang for the first time at Carnegie Hall. Eventually, she decided to go to Europe, where she spent a number of months studying with Charles Cahier before launching a highly successful European singing tour.

In the summer of 1930, she met the Finnish pianist Kosti Vehanen, who became her regular accompanist and her vocal coach for many years. During Anderson's early 1930s touring throughout Europe, she did not encounter the racial prejudices she had experienced in America.

She also met Jean Sibelius through Vehanen after he had heard her in a concert in Helsinki. Moved by her performance, Sibelius invited them to his home and told Anderson that he felt that she had been able to penetrate the Nordic soul. The two struck up an immediate friendship, which further blossomed into a professional partnership, and for many years Sibelius altered and composed songs for Anderson to perform.

Anderson later became the first African American to perform with the Metropolitan Opera in New York. In addition, President Dwight D. Eisenhower appointed her as a delegate to the United Nations Human Rights Committee. The same year, she was elected a Fellow of the American Academy of Arts and Sciences. In 1958, she was officially designated delegate to the United Nations.

On January 20, 1961, she sang for President John F. Kennedy's inauguration, and in 1962, she performed for President Kennedy and other dignitaries in the East Room of the White House. She was active in supporting the civil rights movement during the 1960s, giving benefit concerts for the Congress of Racial Equality; in 1963, she appeared at the March on Washington.

That same year, she was one of the original recipients of the Presidential Medal of Freedom, and she also released her album, *Snoopycat: The Adventures of Marian Anderson's Cat Snoopy*, which included short stories and songs about her beloved black cat. In 1965, she concluded her farewell tour, after which she retired from public performance. The international tour began at Constitution Hall on October 24, 1964, and ended at Carnegie Hall on April 18, 1965.

On January 27, 2005, a commemorative US postage stamp honored Marian Anderson as part of the Black Heritage Series. Anderson is also pictured on the US $5,000 Series 1 United States savings bond.

Food for Thought

WE MUST ALL FIND our place in this world. If we can't look upon these wonderful human beings who gave their lives for us and carry on the rich and brave legacy that they gave us, we will never come to the true nature of our greatness as a people. So ask yourself what society will remember as *your* legacy? Mr. Michael and Ms. C have dedicated the rest of their life to the uplifting all of their people.

In Memory of E. Troy Weaver - Truly One of a Kind

This is the legacy of President Obama through the eyes of a child! The New York Times published the adorable back story about the photo-which has been hanging in the West Wing of the White House for more than three years-on Thursday, and it's quickly become the most-emailed article on the Times' website.

"I WANT TO KNOW if my hair is just like yours," he told Mr. Obama, so quietly that the president asked him to speak again.

Jacob did, and Mr. Obama replied, "Why don't you touch it and see for yourself?" He lowered his head, level with Jacob, who hesitated.

"Touch it, dude!" Mr. Obama said.

As Jacob patted the presidential crown, {White House photographer Pete} Souza snapped.

"So, what do you think?" Mr. Obama asked.

"Yes, it does feel the same," Jacob said.

Notes

Made in the USA
Columbia, SC
14 March 2022